101

Proven Ways to Motivate Athletes

Keith Manos

Note: This book is an updated edition of *101 Ways to Motivate Athletes.*

ISBN: 978-1-60679-541-5
Cover design: Cheery Sugabo
Book layout: Bean Creek Studio
Front cover photos (left to right): © Cliff Welch/Icon SMI via ZUMA Press;
© Jason Moore/ZUMA Wire; John Nepolitan/RunnerSpace

Coaches Choice
P.O. Box 1828
Monterey, CA 93942
www.coacheschoice.com

Dedication

This book is dedicated to my three children—Brittny, John-Morgan, and Christian—who motivate me every day to be the best father I can be.

Acknowledgments

A lifetime of experience typically contributes to the writing of any book, and I am grateful for all the positive experiences I have had as an athlete and coach. I especially appreciate what I learned about competing in sports from my former teammates and coaches at Bay High School and all the coaches I encountered during my tenures as a football, wrestling, and baseball coach. Most importantly, I may never have participated in athletics and then become a coach if not for my older brother Michael who, as a varsity football player and wrestler, was my athletic role model and number one motivator.

Finally, on the publishing side, I am fortunate to work with the dedicated staff of Coaches Choice, especially editor Kristi Huelsing and publisher Dr. Jim Peterson, whose ongoing support and guidance brought this book to publication. I so enjoy working with you all.

Contents

Chapter 4: All Season

Introduction

If every athlete was truly self-motivated, the coach's job would be so much easier. The reality, however, is that even the most talented athletes depend on their coaches to motivate them before, during, and after competitions. Indeed, relatively few athletes will consistently exert maximum effort if they believe that only minimum effort is required to be successful in a competition. That's why experienced coaches, either from direct experience or personal research, recognize the importance of motivating their athletes. They understand that most athletes do not show up at that first practice intensely motivated and ready to compete. In fact, successful coaches typically start motivating their athletes even before the actual season begins and do not take for granted that their athletes are already motivated.

The Association for Applied Sport Psychology says "[t]he key to motivating young athletes is to point out their successes, encourage them to improve, and teach them needed skills." Clearly, coaches need to understand what prompts athletes to participate in their sport and what methods they can employ to motivate athletes through what sports psychologist Dr. Jim Taylor calls "the Grind, which starts when it gets tiring, painful, and tedious. The Grind is also the point at which it really counts.

"The Grind is what separates successful athletes from those who don't achieve their goals. Many athletes when they reach this point either ease up or give up because it's just too darned hard. But truly motivated athletes reach the Grind and keep on going." Coaches also need to recognize how motivation influences athletic performance.

"Motivation is an internal energy force that determines all aspects of our behavior," says researcher Andrew Hamilton in *Motivation and Sport Psychology*. "[I]t also impacts on how we think, feel and interact with others. In sport, high motivation is widely accepted as an essential prerequisite in getting athletes to fulfil their potential. However, given its inherently abstract nature, it is a force that is often difficult to exploit fully." There is, of course, a close connection between motivation and inspiration. I believe that if a coach attempts to do one, they are accomplishing both. Greg Shelley, writing for the Janssen Sports Leadership Center, admits, "No doubt there are many ways to 'motivate' and inspire others. In contrast, it may be argued that one person cannot motivate another but only creates an environment that promotes one to motivate him/ herself. In short, to motivate anyone can be difficult, dynamic, and frustrating. To be effective, motivating others takes insight (a plan) and patience (time)."

"Enhancing motivation is fundamentally about a change of attitude, developing a positive 'can-do' mindset and engaging in systematic behaviors—the short-term process goals—that facilitate improvement," adds Hamilton. "If you have a leadership role in sport, you will have considerable influence on how motivated your athletes or team might feel. You can instill a good work ethic, recognize individual effort and instigate transparent reward structures that reinforce people's sense of competence. To work best, the techniques . . . need to be molded around specific circumstances and the needs of individual athletes."

Motivation to succeed is the most important thing an athlete can have and probably the hardest thing a coach can teach. In "How Coaches Contribute to Athletes' Motivation," Dominique Stasulli says, "An athlete's motivation plays a fundamental role in performance and perceived ability. Motivation comes from internal and external sources, so both nature and nurture contribute to the whole drive of the athlete."

This book offers coaches of all sports proven methods for getting and keeping their athletes motivated, inspired, and on track to experiencing successful seasons.

Preseason

Anutr Yossundara/Shutterstock.com

Model Motivation

As the coach, you should be the most motivated individual on the team and, therefore, should exhibit each day the traits of a motivated person. How you act and what you say should always reflect motivational signals to your athletes—especially what you say. In fact, tell your athletes what motivates you, then model being a motivated person at all times.

The act of motivating is, in its simplest terms, a means of fostering a strong belief in you and your program. You establish this belief by the sincerity of what you say and the intensity of how you say it. Don't misinterpret this to mean you must raise your voice or shake a fist; yelling and histrionics are not signs of effective coaching. "Be present and focused when you coach," says Anne Josephson in her informative article, "15 Ways to Motivate Your Athletes (Backed by Science)." "If you are distracted, so are your athletes. Distraction causes a loss of motivation."

Motivation can, at times, be the kind of *image* you wish to reflect—strong, smart, decisive. You must work at that image, like a public relations firm does for a client corporation. Greg Shelley, writing for the Championship Coaches Network, advises, "If you want someone to put in extra time, you better be putting in extra time. Athletes do what they see. This is why the motivation of the coaching staff is so important and why it is so important to have quality team leaders who can lead by example, be held accountable, and promote a climate of motivation and inspiration."

Plus, you need to work at the *quality* of your image which, in turn, can prompt athletes to:
- Maximize their efforts in practice and games.
- Be enthusiastic about their place on the squad.
- Maintain persistence toward a specified goal.
- Handle obstacles, failures, and criticism without quitting the team.
- Be intense during a competition.
- Improve their physical and mental skills.
- Display a positive attitude.
- Be attentive and alert during practices and contests.
- Express an enjoyment for practicing and competing.
- Work cooperatively with teammates coaches.

The coach is truly a salesman: selling a love for the sport, dialoging about its benefits, inviting athletes to participate, and offering them rewards for that participation. Dr. Alan Goldberg echoes this sentiment in his article "A Coach's Guide to Winning at the Motivation Game." "Good motivators are good salespeople," Goldberg claims. "You have to sell your athletes on hard work and the pursuit of excellence. You have to get them to buy that their sacrifices and sweat are worth the price of the goal." Indeed, coaching is motivating, and motivating younger athletes takes work. That is why *you* probably have to be the most motivated person on the team. Your athletes must see that above all else.

Good motivators are good salespeople.

Research Your Athletes **2**

Coaches must understand that coaching today is more than a practice plan attached to a clipboard, statistics punched into a computer, or a championship plaque placed in a trophy case at the end of the season. To succeed, coaches have to put more effort into researching their own athletes than scouting their opponents. Each season brings new athletes with different backgrounds, experiences, and motivations, even if they are returning letter winners. To motivate them, it is imperative first to research each one individually and, second, to use that information to guide them through a potentially difficult and challenging season. Discover and exploit each athlete's level of aspiration: What are their goals? What are they shooting for? What are their expectations?

"I think to be effective you have to really know your athletes and be able to adapt to the situation to fit the needs of each one," says one Ohio college coach. "Everyone is a little different, and I like seeing how far they can progress." Dr. Alan Goldberg expands on this notion: "The kind of relationship that you develop with each athlete from the beginning of the season will largely determine how motivated that individual will be to learn from and perform for you."

The first and most obvious step is to have brief, informal discussions where you ask each athlete about their interests and background. This is, of course, a more personal and time-consuming way of discovering information, but it often leads to a closer relationship between you and each athlete, which is important if you are going to spend a lot of time together. Ask: Why do you like _____ (fill in the name of your sport)? Does competition excite you? What do you like about practices? What *don't* you like?

These conversations can take place before homeroom, during study halls, or after school in the pre-season. Lunch time is another possibility if the athlete doesn't mind giving up time with friends.

Another way to learn more about potential athletes is to have them complete a brief questionnaire (see Figure 2-1) in their homerooms or advisory group. This survey identifies for the coach an athlete's perceptions of athletic achievement. Do they consider talent more important than attitude, strength more essential than hard work? The results provide a coach with insights into the athlete's view of their own potential to succeed.

You can obtain a basic psychological profile of each athlete with a competitive behavior questionnaire (see Figure 2-2). Results in this instance enable a coach to discern in detail an athlete's mental approach to competition and any anxieties they may have. Scores in the 46-56 range suggest a high level of tension, 36-45 is moderate or average, and athletes who total 35 points or less typically suffer little anxiety about competition.

The next research should focus on your athletes' sources of motivation. A general survey of junior high and senior high athletes indicates the primary reason most young people participate in any sport is for affiliation; that is, they like socializing with others. For others, the key motivation could be an intrinsic need to perform successfully or an extrinsic need to gain rewards. A minority simply enjoy pressure and competition. Use Figure 2-3 to learn more about their personal motivation.

How do athletes stay motivated once the season begins?

As long as they are enjoying the sport (and competitions), sustaining friendships, and achieving some success, they will continue competing, according to a dated study of 8000 athletes ages 10-18 by Martha Ewing and Vern Seefleldt, former professors at Michigan State University. Their study also suggests these athletes will quit if they have accomplished their goal(s), have poor relations with teammates, or experience communication problems with coach.

If motivation is a psychological stimulus that can prompt athletes to perform their best in competitions, then the coach has to begin by studying his athletes for their mental approach to competing. The coach has to analyze the athletes' psyche, including:

filippo giuliani/Shutterstock.com

The primary reason most young people participate in any sport is for affiliation.

- What are their personal interests?
- Why have they chosen to become members of the team?
- How committed are they to the program?
- What has motivated them in the past?
- What motivational strategies have failed them in the past?
- How have they handled adversity in the past?

"If you can identify what drives each athlete, you can help to motivate when needed. One size does not fit all when it comes to motivation, and these internal and external factors can exist together," states Sara Robinson, MA, in her article "Motivating Your Young Athletes" for the National Alliance for Youth Sports. Once coaches accept this responsibility to research their athletes, they are more likely to build strong relationships with them and, in turn, enjoy a loyal following. Plus, you should see a growth in both the self-esteem and physical skills of athletes who will appreciate a coach who sees them as individuals and understands their personalities.

Name _____

Please rate from 1-15 with 1 being the most important item and 15 being the least important the following items in regards to being a successful athlete:

_____Dedication and determination

_____Strength

_____Ability to concentrate

_____Flexibility

_____Good positive mental attitude

_____Talent

_____Intelligence

_____Confidence

_____Competitive drive

_____Quickness and mobility

_____Good physical conditioning

_____Liking the sport (enthusiasm)

_____Ability to cooperate with others

_____Coordination and agility

_____Self-motivation

Figure 2-1. What does it take to be a successful athlete?

Name _____ Date _____

How Competitive Are You?

Circle the number under the choice that best describes you, being sure to respond truthfully to each statement.

Statement	Always	Sometimes	Never
1. I get nervous when people watch me compete.	3	2	1
2. Before a contest I have trouble sleeping.	3	2	1
3. I can't focus after making a mistake.	3	2	1
4. I perform better in practice than a match.	3	2	1
5. I make more mistakes when the score is close.	3	2	1
6. I get angry at myself when I make mistakes in a competition.	3	2	1
7. When a coach yells I lose my focus.	3	2	1
8. I stay focused and positive before any contest.	3	2	1
9. I get easily distracted before a contest.	3	2	1
10. The more challenging the competition, the better I perform.	3	2	1
11. I enjoy competing.	3	2	1
12. I don't like to think about the contest, because it makes me too nervous.	3	2	1
13. I worry a lot about getting injured.	3	2	1
14. I usually feel sick or weak before a contest.	3	2	1
15. I set my own goals for practice and contests.	3	2	1
16. I rarely listen to my coach during a contest.	3	2	1
17. I perform best when I'm nervous or worried.	3	2	1
18. I'm usually disappointed by the outcomes of my competitions.	3	2	1
19. I constantly think about my performance.	3	2	1
20. The butterflies bother me throughout a competition.	3	2	1
21. The bigger the crowd, the more worried or tense I become.	3	2	1
22. I have trouble focusing after an official makes a bad call against me.	3	2	1

Total Score _____

Figure 2-2. Competitive behavior questionnaire

Name _____   Grade _____

Homeroom _____

Address _____

Phone _____   Birthdate _____

1. What has been your greatest commitment to date?

_____

_____

_____

_____

2. What will make this sport fun for you?

_____

_____

_____

_____

3. What could be a great achievement for you this year?

_____

_____

_____

_____

4. What are your personal goals this year?

_____

_____

_____

_____

5. What are you willing to do to accomplish your goals?

_____

_____

_____

_____

6. What motivates you?

_____

_____

_____

_____

Figure 2-3. Survey questions

3 Polish Up Your Facilities

The intent in this instance is to keep facilities clean and attractive. The physical environment of your facility or practice area must be considered for its maximum use and aesthetic appeal. Like new uniforms, an attractive and colorful practice room can itself serve to motivate athletes.

And don't neglect other areas like the weight room (lifting), the school hallways (running), and the conference room (videos). All these rooms should be cleaned and organized before you use them for practice. Either accomplish this yourself or turn in workorders for the custodians.

If need be, use the pre-season to clean, paint, and polish. Consider every area where athletes practice or meet: the practice room, locker room, weight room, classroom. Use volunteers and parents, if possible, to assist you in this. Put up championship banners, signs with the school logo and colors, framed pictures of all-state athletes, and motivational slogans. Consider the lighting, floors, and lockers as well; be sure they are bright, clean, and repaired where needed.

Athletes appreciate and enjoy facilities like this, and their personal motivations increase when they detect the athletic department and their coaches are concerned about the areas where they practice and compete. Accomplishing this may take extra time, effort, and funds, but these expenditures are certainly worth it.

fiphoto/Shutterstock.com

The physical environment of your facility or practice area must be considered for its maximum use and aesthetic appeal.

Design a Media Guide **4**

Another public relations method to motivate players is to design, develop, and distribute a media guide for the local media and community, and you can use free time in the pre-season to accomplish this. A typical media guide provides the following information:

- Facts about the school: address; phone numbers; nickname (e.g., Spartans); colors (e.g., blue and white); and enrollment numbers
- Facts about the school's athletic affiliations: conference (e.g., East Suburban Conference); district or region (e.g., northeast district); division (e.g., Division III); and state (e.g., member of the Ohio High School Athletic Association)
- List of school administrators: superintendent, principal, assistant principal(s), athletic director, school board president and members, and dean(s) of students
- Name of booster club president and officers
- School's logo
- Brief preview of the coming season
- Schedule
- Profile of the head coach and assistant coaches, including the middle school coaches
- Team roster, beginning with senior athletes. Include the pictures of each senior and a photograph of the entire squad, if desired
- Brief history of the program
- List of team record holders (e.g., the best time in the 100 meters)
- Conference championships—year by year
- Sectional championships—year by year
- District/state championships—year by year
- Regional placers and champions—year by year
- Qualifiers to the state tournament, including state placers and champions—year by year
- Team championships—conference, tournaments
- List of other personnel: managers, statisticians, trainers, and cheerleaders

Conclude the media guide with a brief overview of the school—its academic and other extra-curricular programs (drama, student government), the composition of its student body, and its reputation for excellence. On a back page, you can also provide some informative details about the sport (for example, the scoring) and how the team or athletes qualify to the state tournament.

Another public relations method to motivate players is to design, develop, and distribute a media guide for the local media and community.

The intent again is publicity and motivation. To design this media guide, seek help from any school-related personnel, especially those persons involved in graphics and computer technology, and have it ready for distribution at the beginning of the season. Your parents will be impressed with your efforts, and your athletes will be motivated by the professional and serious approach you take to the program and their previous accomplishments.

Design a Team Poster/Calendar **5**

Today's coaches have to realize that their work isn't completed after practice has ended. An added duty that too many coaches leave unattended is publicizing their program. Effective public relations can have a significant influence on team success and the athletes' level of motivation. One way to achieve this is by designing and distributing a team poster/calendar.

The team poster/calendar should have pictures of the team and possibly individual players (if it is a small squad), the season schedule, the school logo and/or mascot, and where and how to buy tickets. One coach at a rural school placed a picture of his players dressed in hunting gear above the caption: "We're in the Hunt for a Championship." Another coach had his wrestlers wear leather jackets and sit on motorcycles to portray an intimidating presence. The stern looks on their faces revealed that they were truly motivated.

Whatever you choose to do, post the team poster/calendar in the school, community businesses and stores, athletes' homes, and city hall. Once community members and parents are aware of all your competition dates and the faces of the players, they may get more excited about the season and even encourage other potential athletes to join the team. These people can spread the word about your team to their relatives, neighbors, and friends and bring them to competitions to make a loud, strong, and united cheering section. They can add enthusiasm to the program, which, in turn, increases the popularity of your sport in the school system and the motivation of your players.

Public relations and advertising are closely connected in this instance. You are a salesman, and your product is your program. Your objective is to attract the attention of the people in your school and community and get them interested in your product. This has become a principal way to motivate athletes. An assistant principal at one Ohio high school told me he looks to hire a coach who has "the right attitude to work with the community, relate well to students and parents, and have some experience in public relations."

Gaining support from an entire community is certainly challenging and, to be sure, often slowly accomplished. Yet, do not be surprised by a snowball effect after you begin your efforts. Your own passion for your program can serve to inspire others to support it and your players. Fostering enthusiasm for your team in both the school and general community may appear as an overwhelming challenge, but this responsibility cannot be neglected, especially if you want to motivate your athletes.

6 Order Cool Clothes

All athletes love new equipment and stylish uniforms. Therefore, if funds are available either through your athletic department or booster club, order some. Invite returning letter winners to submit suggestions or even select the uniforms or warmups they would like to wear the next season. This can be tremendously motivating.

You could also order team hats, T-shirts, hoodies, or sweaters. You might consider ordering jerseys, warmup tops, or sweatshirts that have their names (or nicknames) on the back. Even new socks, gloves, and wristbands are appreciated by athletes.

New uniforms and other apparel can attract attention, enhance performance, and encourage motivation. Moreover, try to purchase uniforms for every level, not just the varsity. Hand-me-downs are hand-me-downs regardless of their age, and younger athletes deserve (fairness!) new equipment as much as the older ones (think liability). Your players will appreciate this and probably perform with greater intensity and motivation during competition.

All athletes love new equipment and stylish uniforms.

Post Slogans 7

Putting motivational slogans and sayings on the walls of the locker room and practice room can potentially inspire some athletes, especially during practice. Dr. Jim Taylor calls these "motivational cues." He adds that a "big part of staying motivated involves generating positive emotions associated with . . . effort and achieving goals. A way to keep those feelings is with motivational cues, such as inspirational phrases and photographs." Taylor tells athletes, "If you come across a quote or a picture that moves you, place it where you can see it regularly such as in your bedroom, on your refrigerator door, or in your locker. Look at it periodically and allow yourself to experience the emotions it creates in you. These reminders and the emotions associated with them will inspire and motivate you to continue to work hard toward your goals."

Feeling exhausted at the mid-point of practice, athletes may look up, see Vince Lombardi's "Fatigue makes cowards of us all" on a poster board, and fight through their exhaustion to finish practice strongly. In fact, the more slogans/sayings you can place on the wall, the better.

Among other examples of motivational cues are the following:
- "The difference between the possible and the impossible lies in the man's determination" (Tommy Lasorda).
- "Do not let what you cannot do interfere with what you can do" (John Wooden).
- "We're good because we work harder than anybody else" (Walter O'Malley).
- "The most certain way to succeed is to always try one more time" (Thomas Edison).

There are, of course, many more. You could obtain a copy of *The Edge* by the late Howard Ferguson, which offers hundreds of quotes from all types of athletes and famous individuals that relate to success in athletics. Ask a sign company or your school art department to put them on boards that can then be nailed into the walls of your workout area. Explain some of the background of each of the individuals who stated the quotes and encourage your players to read them each day. Short, direct, and provocative statements are the most motivating, but any type of motivational slogan can be effective.

8   **Have a Preseason Team Meeting**

A survey of nearly 3100 high schools across the country revealed that 82% of those schools' athletic groups held preseason team meetings. At this point, the tone and tempo of the season are revealed, and a positive first impression is crucial. You have to be prepared for this very important meeting, because it can have a major effect on your players' motivation.

Therefore, be organized and enthusiastic at this first meeting. You must begin on time and quickly establish your credibility. The athletes should learn your background, expectations, and personality through a brief, but detailed, introduction. What the athletes learn about you in this instance, is important, but you also need to learn some things about them. Have them complete a personal data form and a brief questionnaire (see Forms 2-1 and 2-2).

Distribute on paper or display on a white board or screen the agenda of the meeting and be sure that all distractions are eliminated. Introduce assistant coaches and any related personnel (trainers, managers) and clarify their responsibilities and authority.

A discussion about the team's goals and direction should follow. Deal with effort and eligibility, commitment and courage, rules and respect, sacrifice and success. Invite them to contribute ideas about team goals and practices. What are their expectations? What kind of activities have helped them win in the past? What kind of things haven't worked?

Day Of Victory Studio/Shutterstock.com

A preseason team meeting is very important because it can have a major effect on the players' level of motivation.

Also address the importance of motivation to both team and individual success. You can even use Dr. Jim Taylor's comments: "Motivation in sports is so important, because you must be willing to work hard in the face of fatigue, boredom, pain, and the desire to do other things. Motivation will impact everything that influences your sports performance: physical conditioning, technical and tactical training, mental preparation, and general lifestyle including sleep, diet, school or work, and relationships.

"Finally, motivation will impact performance. It is also the only factor over which you have control. Motivation will directly impact the level of success that you ultimately achieve. If you are highly motivated to improve your performances, then you will put in the time and effort necessary. Motivation will also influence the level of performance when you begin a competition. If you're competing against someone of nearly equal skill, it will not be ability that will determine the outcome. Rather, it will be the athlete who works the hardest, who doesn't give up, and who performs his or her best when it counts. In other words, the athlete who is most motivated to win."

Establish that you are in partnership with the athletes, that your primary goal is to empower them to compete successfully. Explain that you are committed to coaching them and that you expect them to be coachable. Be sure to conclude on a positive note and remind them the date, time, and place of the first official practice. This opening meeting has to be as much about inspiration as it does information.

2

Early Season

JoeSAPhotos/Shutterstock.com

Show Enthusiasm 9

Clearly, you have to have enjoy coaching and working with athletes. You show this with enthusiasm, a behavior that displays eagerness, intensity, and zeal. Former United States President Harry Truman makes a simple claim: "The successful man has enthusiasm . . . Every great achievement is the story of a flaming heart." The athletes, in turn, should recognize your excitement and self-confidence and will hopefully feel compelled to match your energy and attitude.

Enthusiasm can often prompt athletes to believe in you, especially through those difficult periods (losses), when you appear unmoved by any setback. Furthermore, create an enthusiastic atmosphere in the practice room and the locker room, so that the athletes know you are concerned for their welfare and passionate about their success. The ancient Egyptian scholar Papyrus wrote, "Enthusiasm must be nourished with new actions, new aspirations, new efforts, new vision."

The coach's enthusiasm prompts athletes to act on their own personal motivations. Even 19th century essayist Ralph Waldo Emerson recognized that "[n]othing great was ever accomplished without enthusiasm."

Enthusiasm can often prompt athletes to believe in their coach.

Rawpixel.com/Shutterstock.com

10 Develop Team Pride

Newcomers to your program may be totally unfamiliar with both their new teammates and the team's history. Therefore, motivate them (and the entire group) by speaking about team pride. You have to nurture a winning attitude and pride in the program. The following are eight strategies that you can employ:

- Be sure each athlete knows his value to the team.
- Point out how the team has succeeded in the past.
- Use terms like *"Our* team . . ." and *"We*'re on track . . ."
- Highlight team accomplishments.
- Discuss regularly the team's goals.
- Show them trophies, banners, or videos that   document your sport's success in previous seasons.
- Frequently refer to the team logo/nickname, school colors, and school name.

In addition, you should reward athletes for assisting and encouraging each other. On occasion, this is termed "team chemistry." The Association for Applied Sport Psychology in the "Motivating Young Athletes" article recommends that coaches foster "team cohesion." Develop this through presenting regular team building activities, like those listed in the "30 Team Building Activities for Sports" on the Signup Genius website. Coaches should also offer opportunities for players to have appropriate social interactions.

According to Sara Robinson, "When teammates are close (or even when an individual has one close friend on a team), and relationships are strong, motivation has been shown to increase. *What can you do?* Take time to help teammates get to know each other, have activities outside of training, or maybe have team buddies for a holiday or birthdays. You can combine several of these ideas by asking the team how they would like to celebrate the birthdays of team members (this would enhance feelings of control and connectedness)."

Other methods for establishing team camaraderie include the following:

When the team assembles on the first day of practice form a close circle and deal with three questions:

- Why are you here?
- What do you want to accomplish this season?
- What is one personal item you can share with us?

This question-answer process takes about 20-40 minutes (depending on the size of your team) and usually involves some serious thought on their part (e.g., how often are athletes required to voice their goals to teammates?), especially by the younger players who may not be certain yet what they want to accomplish. More importantly, everyone listens. As the returning lettermen speak, the newcomers learn why the sport is enjoyable and what is possible for them.

For each question, answers vary, of course, yet there is a common thread that connects all responses. Their answers to the first question often reflect their need to be part of a group. One study reveals that this need to socialize, called "affiliation," is the primary factor for many athletes joining a particular team. Accordingly, young people seem to consider gaining friendship as more important than achieving awards. Typical responses in this instance are, "Because my friend is on the team," "I don't like football, and cross country is perfect for guys like me," and "It looks like fun."

Teenagers, by nature, are often idealistic. This becomes quite evident when they respond to question #2. You may hear the following:
- "Be champions of the conference."
- "Get in great shape."
- "Go undefeated."

Obviously, these types of comments reflect players' high expectations for the team, and from this, a *group* attitude toward team success emerges. They may discover that many of them have the same goal: they all want to have a winning, competitive team.

When teammates are close and relationships are strong, motivation has been shown to increase.

The coach can also infer that they want practices to be intense, yet enjoyable. Through their own words, they have become unified toward a common purpose and outcome: challenging practices and a successful season.

For the final question, it may be as brief as "Where do you live?" or "What's your favorite movie?" or something more complex like "What's the craziest thing you've ever seen in this school?" or "How would you define courage?" Some good-natured teasing may occur, but humor helps ease the tension some of the athletes may feel about beginning a new season. Be sensitive, of course, to their socioeconomic and cultural backgrounds. For instance, questions about dating or parents could embarrass some kids.

Your input as a coach to this point has been minimal. The athletes have done all the talking, even most of the decision-making, especially regarding team goals. You have simply directed whose turn it is to speak next.

An athlete's intrinsic motivation improves when they sense being "in control." Conversely, if they have little or no control, they tend to be less motivated. Offer them control from day one; share responsibility with them by using this Q & A approach at the first practice.

Don't misunderstand. Don't ignore your status as team leader. You still must make many decisions in consultation with your coaching staff. However, the athletes can be involved in many issues regarding team objectives and direction, as in the following:

- Scheduling: "We have a choice of three tournaments next year. Which one would you like to compete in?"
- Motivation: "Guys, I'm not giving the pep talk today. You are. Jenny, tell Jill what she needs to do today to win her tennis match."
- Technique: "Rachel, show us how you set yourself before you go to spike the ball."
- Finally, and possibly most important, coaches must make consistent references to the team's accomplishments both in practice and competitions. One of America's greatest coaches, the legendary John Wooden, succinctly emphasizes this point: "The main ingredient of stardom is the rest of the team."

Describe Success   **11**

Some athletes just want to say that they are a member of the team. They may care only a little about being successful and don't want to be responsible for the team losing. In this way, these underachievers can avoid blame or criticism. An important duty for a coach, then, is to prepare athletes to triumph, especially those kids who only have infrequent experiences with success. All coaches need to define and describe success for athletes to motivate them to pursue both team and individual success.

Start with yourself first. A winning coach sets high standards and succeeds because they expect to succeed. When a negative belief enters their mind (for example, "We just can't run the ball against anyone") they quickly replace it with a positive one ("Okay then, we're going to be the best team in the conference at passing"). This may appear to be a Pollyanna-ish approach, but this mind set is characteristic of all successful people. This type of outlook on a practical level requires the coach to:

1. Analyze your situation, for example, the team has difficulty running the football.
2. Design an advantage for example, we'll work harder on passing the ball.
3. Believe enthusiastically that the plan will succeed for example, we'll total more passing yardage than our opponents in every conference game.

Furthermore, describe success clearly and concisely to the entire coaching staff and then the team. You might, for instance, read out loud several dictionary definitions or use quotes from famous individuals, for example:

- "You are never better than anyone else until you do something to prove it, and when you are really good, you never need to tell anyone. They will tell you." (Ken Venturi, former professional golfer and sports broadcaster)
- "A real champion must learn to handle success, which in some ways is even more difficult than dealing with defeat." (Don Schollander, five-time Olympic Gold Medalist in swimming)

Ask players: What determines, for instance, a successful athlete in _____ (insert name of your sport)? What makes up a successful high school golfer? Or a winning football team? Or a champion gymnast?

Defining success and discussing strategy with players each day (3-4 minutes) affirms their acceptance of those standards and enhances their motivation. Then relate to them how their practice activities help lead to success, for example, as a golfer, a football team, or a gymnast. Completing these activities in practice with enthusiasm and diligence becomes everyone's priority. Repetition of these affirmations leads to mastery. It also keeps your players focused.

You can even help your players visualize success. For example, one football coach took his team in full uniform during the first week of practice to the stadium where the state championship game would be held eighteen weeks later and put them through their pre-game warm up as if they were to play the game that day. A wrestling coach makes his wrestlers stand on a victory podium and plays recorded cheering as if they have just won a tournament. A golf coach shows a video of professional golfers, one after another, sinking amazing putts. A baseball coach has season tickets to Cleveland Indians games and takes 2-3 players to each game and comments on the skills of the players on the field. Their intent is simple: Here is what success feels like and looks like; let's make it happen for us.

Most coaches already have the basic characteristics of a winning, competitive personality. They know how to present themselves as positive and successful individuals. When a coach responds to their athletes in the same way, the athletes will be more motivated.

But there is more for you to do to help athletes accept your definition of success. You need to have faith that *they* can be successful. The following are quotes from high school athletes on this subject:

- "The coach has to believe in me and give me a chance."
- "My performance improved because my coach had faith in me."
- "My coach kept pushing me to greater achievements and setting even higher goals."
- "Our strength and conditioning coach made the greatest difference for me. [He] made me run and lift weights when I didn't want to. At times I thought he was a jerk. Now, I have the utmost respect for this man. I can honestly say I owe all my success to him."

Jacob Lund/Shutterstock.com

All coaches need to define and describe success for athletes to motivate them to pursue both team and individual success.

Praise Athletes the Right Way 12

All athletes want to know if they are pleasing the coach, both in practice and during competition. Indeed, all athletes desire praise, and many constantly need feedback about their progress and their performance. A four-time state wrestling champion I coached needed some form of praise every day.

To be sure, for all athletes, praise should begin at the start of the season. First, simply praise them for choosing to participate in your sport; then keep on praising them as the season progresses by finding as many opportunities and reasons to do so. Praise any positive scrimmage/practice results, exceptional behavior, and/or diligent effort (hustle).

Keep in mind that how you praise them at the beginning of the season should differ from the statements used near the middle or end of the season. Your athletes may see the praise as insincere if it resembles what they have heard all along (e.g., you sound more like a broken tape recorder than a pleased coach). Also, know when to offer praise to the team and when only individuals deserve it. Just be sure they know *why* they are being praised when you do so.

When deciding to praise an individual athlete, timing and location are crucial. "For example," says Sara Robinson, a mental skills coach who has a masters in sports psychology, "one player may appreciate getting positive feedback: it helps her understand what she needs to work on, but she doesn't like being praised in front of the group. You may think you're encouraging her by giving positive feedback, but she may actually experience a drop in motivation when she gets this feedback in front of the team. Take the time to notice how your players react to situations like these."

The coach should provide specific information about performances (practice or competition) to athletes routinely, especially the ones who have set their own training goals. This constant assessment (beyond generic commentary, for example, like "You did a nice job today" or "You had a good practice") encourages athletes to set personal standards for their practice and, hence, the competition. Better, more specific, compliments would be, "You never stopped hustling during drills today. You're setting a standard I'd like everyone to follow. Well done!" or "Your form and follow-through on your jump shot are excellent. Do it that way all the time, and no one will stop you from scoring."

In fact, players should be given some indication of their improvement after each practice. At issue in this instance, is the type of praise you give athletes. Know when to praise a little and when to praise a lot. You should recognize that too much praise lessens the impact, value, and sincerity of your message. Concentrate on specific praise, which promotes independent action, when individuals deserve it, and generic praise to prompt the entire team to act in a certain manner. Coaches should especially be ready to praise when they observe athletes' showing improvement in their skill level and during competition.

According to Dominique Stasulli in her article "How Coaches Contribute to Athletes' Motivation," "[w]ithout guidance, encouragement, and positive feedback from the coaches, athletes may experience discouragement, lack of motivation, unwarranted anxieties, and burnout." Moreover, the Association for Applied Sport Psychology declares, "Athletes will be more confident as the coach points out their improvements and successes." Clearly, effectively expressed praise can have a strong impact on any athlete's motivation.

When deciding to praise an individual athlete, timing and location are crucial.

digitalskillet/Shutterstock.com

Promote Team Leaders 13

Discover and then promote team leaders. Keep in mind, however, these athletes don't necessarily have to be captains. The truth is that during any practice or competition, athletes look to their peers for leadership as much as they do their coaches. In fact, the best team leaders, or team captains, are, in a way, an extension of the coaching staff. They help determine the team's goals and share the responsibilities of team management and motivation.

I recommend caution and reflection when considering who should be your team leaders. As stated by Joe Namath, "To be a leader, you have to make people want to follow you, and nobody wants to follow someone who doesn't know where he is going."

Effective team leaders may not be the ones who lift the most weight on the bench press exercise or yell the loudest during drills. Most often, the best team leaders are players who have earned the most respect and have shown the most dependability. This athlete arrives early for practice ready to learn and often stays afterwards to master a technique. They never complain when problems occur and remains positive about the outcome of any contest. Both the coach and the team can count on this person.

At the beginning of the season, therefore, seek out two to three athletes who have a take-charge attitude and a high level of commitment. They are usually veterans who believe in the program and understand and respect your coaching philosophy. Ask them privately if they'd be interested in serving as team leaders, but clarify that this request is only exploratory, not a final decision. Plus, they should feel no pressure to accept this offer.

A private discussion is best, because if you thrust leadership on any individual (maybe the player who had the best performance the previous season), the results could be disastrous. This action could cause this athlete to experience too much pressure, and they may resent you for it. You might offer leadership status to an individual on a temporary basis and later decide together if you both are satisfied.

One week of practice is usually adequate to identify those athletes who have the potential to serve as captains. They've been punctual, coachable, and reliable. In short, they are highly motivated and set the example younger athletes should emulate.

Announce to the team during that week that the coaches are looking for team leaders and expecting at least several players to show an interest. Explain the entire selection process to the team so there are no misunderstandings or surprises (fairness!). The next step is to ask them on the chosen day (at least one day later) to declare in front of their teammates their desire to be captains.

The most successful captains *want* to be leaders! In this instance, usually at the end of the practice, each athlete stands and in turn announces their reasons for wanting to be a captain. It is possible other candidates could surface at this time or that an original choice could change their mind. If the squad is large with over, for example, 50 participants, then 3-4 captains are acceptable; for smaller teams, 1-2 captains are sufficient. Keep in mind that too many captains can affect team unity and motivation while a single leader could set up an autocracy that could make some athletes feel uncomfortable and unmotivated. After these one-minute speeches, the team votes on paper ballots, which are tabulated later by the coaching staff.

It could happen that the team selects an athlete you deem unworthy after time; nevertheless, do not interfere with the balloting. The trust you have with the athletes and the acceptance the new captains need from them could be ruined if you do this. Indeed, you may ruin the motivation you are trying to create.

Announce the captains at the beginning of the next practice and meet with the new captains afterwards. At this meeting, explain you are in partnership with them, that your primary goal is to empower them and the team to compete successfully, and that you expect them to be coachable. They should work to make both themselves and their teammates better players. Be sure they have a clear understanding of their responsibilities, which include the following:

*Most often, the best team leaders are players who have earned
the most respect and have shown the most dependability.*

- recruiting more athletes into the sport
- helping maintain discipline in the locker room
- leading by example
- eliminating any hazing of younger athletes
- leading the warmup before practice and matches
- helping determine strategy for the next opponent
- deciding the uniform to be worn (if you have several) for a competition
- communicating effectively with both teammates and the coaching staff at all times
- addressing any grievances with the coaches
- occasionally running practice

Give these captains meaningful responsibilities and include them in matters that involve disciplinary measures. Moreover, avoid treating them as servants. Allow them, in fact, opportunities to address teammates ("captain's talks") either before or after practices. After the first meeting with the team leaders, the coaching staff can finalize all plans for the coming season.

Continue to monitor the new captains. Remind them to show genuine interest in the other athletes' welfare to make them feel they are not just another spoke in the wheel on the team.

If, during the season, a team leader looks like a champion one day and a chump the next, discuss this with them. For erratic performers like this, the underlying problem is often a fear of not measuring up, either in competitions or as a leader. Serving as a team leader may have expanded a feeling of pressure for them and hindered their motivation. You can lessen this pressure by pointing out their successes in contests and their positive influences on the younger athletes. Clarify your interest in their effort, not their wins and losses.

Finally, make sure your staff is prepared to work with these team leaders during the season. Each coach should know the captains' responsibilities and respect their position as leaders. In this way, the team leaders can feel confident and motivated. When you demonstrate confidence in these individuals, you discover the power of using team leaders, and the team's motivation improves.

14 Be Organized

You've heard the old cliché: Failing to plan is planning to fail. And, in truth, the statement is especially appropriate to the coaching profession. "No matter how naturally gifted an athlete or team may be, the coach without a plan for the development of those talents will usually fail to unlock their full potential," says Geoff Gowan, former national track and field coach for England, Puerto Rico, and Canada. An Ohio high school principal adds: "When I hire a coach, I look for someone who has a concern for students and good coaching skills, and I especially consider their organizational skills."

Many studies have indicated that coaches (and teachers) who regularly show confidence in their abilities have a stronger influence on their athletes (or students). "Leadership is a matter of having people look at you and gain confidence by seeing how you react," says former NFL Dallas Cowboys head coach Tom Landry. "If you show you're in control, they're in control."

Before beginning any activity that involves a group which is directed toward a certain goal(s), you need to get organized. Athletes are motivated, in part, by a coach who is organized and prepared. A coach's organizational duties include:

- Planning a daily practice schedule
- Getting directions for all away competitions (to distribute to parents later)
- Arranging for guest clinicians or coaches
- Doing an inventory of uniforms and equipment (use your athletic department's supplies request form to order necessary equipment)
- Arranging for scrimmages with other schools
- Arranging for games to be videotaped by a parent or assistant coach
- Determining and designing Player of the Week awards (a T-shirt, certificate, trophy)
- Consulting with the athletic director about their expectations for the team and the use of the school facilities through the season

Whether you coach a YMCA team or a Division I college program, the obligations and functions for proper team management are the same. Athletes require and deserve a structured and disciplined approach by the coach. Practices cannot be planned haphazardly. Your players need to know what to expect and how to respond to the activities the coaching staff plans. In this way, the athletes are motivated because they see the organized coach as the catalyst to help them realize their potential.

Athletes are motivated, in part, by a coach who is organized and prepared.

The time allotted for practice, the competition schedule, and the length of the season can determine the activities you plan for your athletes. In that regard the following basic fundamentals should be considered:

- Every practice needs to have specific objective(s).
- Athletes need to know clearly the reasons for accomplishing those objectives.
- Practice should never be punishment.
- Unless injured, all athletes should be participating all the time during practice.
- Practice should be an enjoyable and challenging experience.

Former NFL Pittsburgh Steelers head coach Chuck Knox commented on the need for organization quite effectively: "Always have a plan and believe in it. Nothing good happens by accident—it happens because of good organization. There must be a plan for everything, and the plan will prevent you from overlooking little things. By having that plan, you'll be secure, and self-doubts will never become a factor."

Remember that administrators have expectations of you as well. For Richard Corbin, a former administrator at Griswold (CT) Senior High School, a coach's evaluation depends on several factors. "The four key components I look for in a coach," says Corbin, "are his strength as a motivator, an innovator, a communicator, and an organizer. We want to know whether a coach hands in thier paperwork on time, meets deadlines, . . . and runs an efficient practice."

John Wooden was even more succinct: "Without organization and leadership toward a realistic goal, there is no chance of realizing more than a small percentage of your potential." Effective organization not only gives a foundation and a sense of direction for your program, it also leads to motivation.

15 Have a "Meet the Team" Event

Host a "Meet the Team" night at the beginning of the season the week before the first game. Invite athletes, managers, statisticians, coaches, administrators, fans, faculty, the media, students, and parents to this evening program.

Most parents are pleased when their child decides to join an interscholastic sport, and they are even more pleased when they can see their child acknowledged in front of their peers. The "Meet the Team" event, best held on a weekday evening, can motivate both players and their parent/guardians.

A typical agenda for this event should take no more one to one and a half hours. You, as the head coach, should do the following:

- Welcome those who attend and thank them for their recognition of the importance of the "Meet the Team" night event.
- Introduce the managers and acknowledge them for their daily contributions to the program.
- Have the advisor to the statisticians introduce these individuals and clarify their duties during games.
- Introduce your coaching staff and give the key backgrounds of each coach. Allow each coach to say a few words, if they are comfortable with speaking to a large group.
- Explain the coaching staff's philosophy, goals, and expectations for each of the freshmen, junior varsity, and varsity squads. You should also explain your expectations of parents, which usually centers on the kind of behavior they should display in the stands (sportsmanship, enthusiasm).
- Comment briefly on typical practice activities. Some coaches invite the parents to an actual practice.
- Display a slide show or video of the athletes in action in practice or at a scrimmage.
- Allow a special guest speaker(s) to make a presentation to the parents and athletes in this situation. Some possibilities here would be a sports psychologist, physical therapist, college coach or athlete, a licensed nutritionist, and an experienced mother of a varsity athlete.
- Invite the athletic director or principal to speak to the group.
- Distribute an information packet that includes the practice and competition schedule, nutrition guide, and training rules.

- Introduce, in order, the freshmen, junior varsity, and varsity teams, or organize the introduction by classes, beginning with freshmen and ending with seniors. Possibly allow the team captains to make a brief comment on their expectations for the season.
- Conclude by thanking the fans and parents and offering your hope that the season will be a pleasant and memorable experience for them. Invite everyone to stay for any informal discussions and refreshments (ask some parents to arrange this for you).

The bottom line is that athletes enjoy being first introduced and then publicly praised by their coach(es). They may feel even more motivated when they see parent/guardians, administrators, and others recognizing the importance of their participation in the sport. The "Meet the Team" event can serve to begin the season on a positive note and to send some strong motivational messages.

The "Meet the Team" event can serve to begin the season on a positive note and to send some strong motivational messages.

16 Create a Display Case

Think color, pictures, logo, and names, and you're on the right track to designing a display case that can motivate athletes. You should display your players and their accomplishments for all to see. Hopefully, you can utilize a display case in a prominent and well-traveled area of the school. In short, celebrate both team and individual success.

Ask art students or the art teacher to assist you, if necessary, and make the display colorful (your school colors) and bright (lighting). Place the athletes' pictures and the team roster, the school logo, your competition schedule, and last season's accomplishments inside the display.

As the season progresses, post news articles about your team and additional pictures, trophies, and/or banners. Some coaches have put Athlete of the Week Awards, motivational slogans, team T-shirts, and small banners in a display case to highlight their team and motivate their athletes. Either way, be sure to be cautious about overloading a small case or neglecting any member of the team.

Think color, pictures, logo, and names, and you're on the right track to designing a display case that can motivate athletes.

Establish Rules 17

For any team to be successful, a group effort is required. Therefore, group rules are needed. The individual athlete, in turn, becomes responsible to the group. Rarely are athletes motivated when rules are either vague or ignored. Norm Van Brocklin, a former NFL quarterback and coach, emphasizes that "if you don't discipline them, they won't know you love them. There's no love on third down and one. You need discipline then."

Researchers indicate that when rules are perceived as a way to punish, they only serve to pressure athletes, not motivate them. Effective rules, on the other hand, get athletes ready to handle the stress of competition. These rules are seen as a positive, almost beneficial influence in the athlete's life. Stephan Terebienic competed in varsity football and wrestling at St. Edward (OH) High School, where he earned an individual state title. He credited his success to coaches who were "tough, strict, and demanding." Disciplined athletes are easy to coach because they follow team and school rules and make themselves accessible to instruction.

Call this psychological conditioning. Every time any kind of group comes together, rules and guidelines need to be established. In that regard, coaches would be wise to:
- Begin psychological conditioning (motivation) on the first day.
- Explain what behavior is acceptable and what isn't.
- Reward behavior that leads to successful performances.
- Get the athletes to believe that the rules are important.
- Modify inappropriate behavior individually but continually stress that you are operating under the premise of what is best for the team and the program.

Rules are simply the standards by which the group is going to operate. On occasion, the size of that group determines these standards. Consider for a moment the coach who trains five athletes and the coach who trains fifty. Both will have different responsibilities for their athletes and different needs. Each has to consider if their rules are just a means to maintain order, if they are to restrict unwanted behavior, or if negative consequences apply only to certain actions.

Former NFL Coach Bud Grant says: "When making decisions, there are three things you have to watch out for. The first is that you can never be afraid of what the critics will think or say. The second is not to make decisions too soon. If you make them before you have to, you'll have a hard time changing your decision should new information, subsequently becomes available to you. The third is that when your decision is to make a rule, you had better be prepared to enforce it. If you are not, then don't make the rule."

There may even be differences between the rules you establish for practice and those you have for competitions. The punishment or reward system has to be carefully developed with both the school's administration and athletes' parents in mind.

What kind of rules do you need? There are certainly those sport-specific rules (like no fouling in basketball) that you must follow, but you need additional guidelines for players to adhere to that govern their behavior and conduct as members of your team, for example:

- Attendance and punctuality at meetings, practice, and competitions, including arriving on time for meetings, practices, and competitions (especially when transportation to another site is involved).
- Caring for uniforms and equipment and replacing any lost or damaged equipment.
- Being cooperative with teammates and coaches.
- The acceptable behavior at practice and during competition, along with respecting all coaches, teammates, officials, opponents, and other school personnel.
- Properly treating locker room facilities (home and away).
- Being attentive to instructions.
- Getting a coach's permission before exiting practice or leaving the site of a competition.
- Abstaining from all nonprescription drugs, alcohol, and tobacco (all types).
- Reporting any injury immediately to a coach.
- Adhering to other rules mandated by the athletic department, especially those about eligibility (academics).

When athletes respond in disciplined fashion, they should be rewarded, which keeps them motivated. When they don't, their actions need to be addressed: How have those actions hurt the team, the athlete, or the coach? The player deserves an explanation, and a goal-oriented team deserves to have that distraction removed. "The coach should always have control and attention of his team," says Gavin Peterson who played on three varsity teams for University (HI) High School. "A coach should always stress discipline. He should not only make his players better players but better people at the same time."

When players violate team rules, the coaching staff must be prepared to administer consequences. Never use a physical activity as a form of punishment. If you use, for instance, sprints at the end of practice, it is possible the players will then equate sprints, which are an effective form of conditioning, with punishment and never run them with intensity. The same factor holds true with any other physical activity (one coach made his athletes compete in 10-12 extra wrestling matches after practice if they got caught chewing gum in school, which made them both stop chewing gum and start hating matches).

Instead, design consequences that not only benefit the athlete but also the entire team. The following are all examples of activities they could do if they've violated a team policy:

- Mop and clean the locker room.
- Pick up any trash in the work out room, gym, and locker room.
- Scrub and disinfect equipment.
- Clean the training room floor, tables, and equipment.
- Clean a classroom(s).

If an athlete still does not change their behavior or actions, you would be wise to have a conference with that individual and their parents. Violations cannot be allowed to continue. These kinds of disruptions hinder everyone's opportunity (motivation) to achieve success.

"Don't be afraid to remind any players who are out of line or not in the spirit of your training rules that they owe it to the school to straighten themselves out," says Paul Brown, legendary NFL coach and general manager. "You win when everyone works together as a team—never let one or two players pull your whole team down."

In short, establish rules for the good of the team, and then follow them. Keep in mind when you devise your rules, that the punishment should be based on the behavior, not on the individual involved. Regardless of major or minor violations, rules have to be handled fairly, consistently, and as soon after the infraction as possible.

During the course of the season, you may have to deal with stealing, fighting, obscenity, lost equipment, and lack of effort. Positive reinforcement for following rules often works better than negative reinforcement when rules are violated. These rules (and how they affect your athletes' motivation) should be evaluated as the season progresses. Players should be praised regularly for adhering to the adopted rules, which can motivate them to continue to remain attentive to team rules and regulations.

18 Avoid Coercion

Read what several athletes have to say about this issue:

- "I don't get motivated by coaches who are always angry. They have to be fun at times, and they have to be a friend."
- "To motivate me, the coach has to be able to give constructive criticism and encouragement, not sarcasm."
- "He should talk in an encouraging manner instead of yelling. He should only talk positive."

The point? Never use physical coercion or verbal threats as motivators. These methods only demonstrate how important team success is for *you,* not the athletes. In the short term, you could increase their efforts in practice, but in the long term, you will only make them bitter and tense about competing. Dr. Alan Goldberg says, "A challenge is positive and motivational. A threat is negative and gets the athlete preoccupied with the consequences for failing."

Negative talk happens most often after the team has lost a competition when coaches want to vent either their frustration, disappointment, or both. Many coaches favor a brief lecture in the locker room or on the bus, where the game is analyzed and performances discussed, especially if the results are below expectations. However, after any competition, especially one that has been exhausting or disappointing, most athletes care little for any commentary.

Axel Alvarez/Shutterstock.com

Never use physical coercion or verbal threats as motivators.

If you must talk to the team, make it only a quick, objective analysis of the competition and make only positive comments; if they've performed badly, they'll know it. Use this moment only to remind them of the next day's schedule (the time of practice or the next match) and to congratulate the performance of any individual(s). Remain positive after a competition (and prompt the players to stay positive, too).

Over time, you'll get better results if you praise and reward rather than criticize and punish. Remember to be realistic about your expectations of your athletes. And if any part of your motivation includes a promised reward—a pizza dinner, for example—for a victory, then be sure to follow through on it promptly.

Coaches must be especially attentive towards the ways they treat their athletes during practices and matches, especially after a loss. Many of today's coaches may have grown up in an era where their coaches used discipline and punishment to motivate athletes, but that style is rarely tolerated today. According to William Beausay, former president of the Academy of Sports Psychology International in Columbus, Ohio, coaches who intimidate or threaten athletes should not be allowed to continue coaching. Beausay also points out that today's young athletes won't tolerate abusive coaches, because they are much more independent than their counterparts in previous decades.

When coaches physically or mentally abuse their athletes, their behavior "borders on pathological," says Frank Smoll, a professor of psychology at the University of Washington. Smoll feels that the more effective coaches utilize a liberal amount of rewards, reinforcements, and praise, as opposed to those who lean toward punitive measures to influence their players' performances.

In summary, as recommended by The Association for Applied Sport Psychology, coaches should "[m]inimize punishment or criticism—this does not mean to ignore mistakes; rather use instruction and encouragement to help athletes improve."

19 Remain Positive

James "Doc" Counsilman, a former United States Olympic swim coach and head swim coach at Indiana University, regularly motivated his swimmers by maintaining a positive attitude around them. He made sure they recognized the progress they were making towards their goals, and he worked hard to build their self-esteem. His swimmers, in turn, felt secure in their positions on the team and welcomed all challenges.

This approach should be duplicated with all athletes. If you keep reminding your athletes of their goal(s) and their accomplishments, they will be more likely to handle any obstacle, failure, or criticism they confront during the season. When they know that they will always hear positive feedback from you, they will be more loyal to you and more likely to be excited about the next competition. A coach should remain positive, especially through setbacks (losses, injuries, complaints). The coach should see setbacks these as steppingstones, not stumbling blocks, to future success.

That was Devin Onwugbufor's approach. Onwugbufor, a Maize (KS) High School wrestler, was born with one leg five inches shorter than the other. He endured six surgeries during his freshmen year and tore his ACL a year later, missing his entire sophomore season. He has only four toes on each foot, and on the second day of practice his senior year, he tore his meniscus. He returned to the line-up after missing two months and suffered a 2-1 loss in the finals of the regional tournament. Through

A coach should remain positive, especially through setbacks (losses, injuries, complaints).

all these setbacks, Devin's determination to be a state champ never wavered, however, and he avenged that loss in the state final to become a 2018 Class 5A state champion. "I've choked too many times before this, so I knew it was my time," Devin says. Indeed, he remained positive about his potential to be successful.

Coaches can even encourage their athletes, as suggested by Andrew Hamilton in *Motivation and Sport Psychology*, to use positive self-talk, "a technique that can be used to enhance motivation across a wide range of achievement domains. It makes use of an athlete's powerful inner voice to reinforce their self-esteem or important aspects of their performance. With appropriate repetition, self-talk can positively alter an athlete's belief system." The late champion boxer Muhammad Ali, in fact, vocalized his positive self-talk when he declared, "I am the greatest." He said later, "I figured that, if I said it enough, I would convince the world that I really was the greatest."

Related to this are visualization exercises—in which, for example, athletes are directed to visualize themselves in scenarios where they are successful, like crossing the finish line first, pinning an opponent in a wrestling match, or catching a touchdown pass. Norman Vincent Peale, a clergyman and noted expert on positive thinking, claims that if an athlete "can mentally visualize and affirm and reaffirm [their] assets . . ., emphasizing them to the fullest extent, [they] will rise out of any difficulty regardless of what it may be."

Maintaining an optimistic outlook, therefore, about the season and the team can make your athletes' memories of you as their coach positive ones as well. Competing under you will have been a satisfying experience, something they can then share with the athletes who follow them.

Some coaches may feel that negative reinforcement can motivate athletes. This factor is true only rarely. Dr. Alan Goldberg calls this a "demotivator." Athletes like being challenged, not criticized. If a coach takes a negative tone with their athlete, then "the relationship is damaged," says Anne Josephson in "15 Ways to Motivate Your Athletes (Backed by Science)," and the athlete's motivation lessens.

When you detect athletes with poor self-images, help them remove any negative beliefs. Remind them daily that they are competent, successful athletes and force that message into their minds. Tell your athletes in practice how they're getting better, that their training has made them stronger, quicker, and more skilled, in order to reaffirm positive self-images. This entire process may take time, maybe an entire season, but it is time well spent. Former NFL coach John Ralston makes a great point with "Success comes in cans, not cannots."

20 Appoint Mentors

Oprah Winfrey says, "A mentor is someone who allows you to see the hope inside yourself." Our athletes, especially the younger ones, need mentors. Mentors can be ministers, teachers, other coaches, former varsity players, community members who are invested stakeholders in your program, or even a senior athlete for a freshman.

Having athletes work with a mentor (hopefully on a daily or weekly basis) can contribute to their psychological and physical development. The athlete's motivation and self-discipline improve when a mentor provides inspiration and guidance. Each player can learn from the mentor the physical and mental skills needed to succeed at that sport and in life. As a noted American educator, Lyman Bryson knows the value of mentorship. "Education is anything that we do," he says, "for the purpose of taking advantage of the experience of someone else."

One of my wrestler's mentors was a former state champion who mentored and trained him four days a week during weightlifting sessions and shared phone calls other days. At my previous school, two female English teachers mentored one wrestler on his academics, relationships, and diet and then attended his competitions to cheer for him. A youth pastor was a mentor to stepbrothers, and he regularly took them out to dinner and to the library where they selected books on famous athletes to read. All these mentors focused on getting their mentee athletes physically and mentally ready for their upcoming competitions.

Shawn Hine,/Shutterstock.com

Having athletes work with a mentor (hopefully on a daily or weekly basis) can contribute to their psychological and physical development.

Before pairing up mentors with members of your team, you should review the mentor's attitude and goals. Find out their personal background and relationship with the athlete and discuss with them their intents (conferring with the athlete's parent/guardian would also be wise). How does the mentor know that athlete? How do they plan to assist the athlete? How regularly can they meet with the athlete? How does their approach to training (physical and mental prep) compare to yours? What is their knowledge/familiarity with the athlete's sport?

Overall, mentors must be supportive, encouraging, and caring, and their priority must be the success of the athlete. If the mentor prioritizes the mentee's physical training and mental approach to the sport and season, then you can expect to see a motivated competitor in practice and in matches. Furthermore, the athlete is more likely to recover more quickly from a poor performance.

If you remain uncertain about using adult mentors for your athletes, one type of mentoring system is to have more mature (senior) athletes act as mentors for younger ones. Another is to link freshmen with freshmen, sophomores with sophomores, etc. The second option tends to match up players who know each other better and might, in fact, be friends outside the team. Either way gives athletes a sense of responsibility to themselves and their teammates; plus, they feel motivated to live up to their mentor's expectations. "Show me a successful individual," says Denzel Washington, "and I'll show you someone who had real positive influences in his or her life. I don't care what you do for a living — if you do it well, I'm sure there was someone cheering you on or showing the way. A mentor."

21 Establish Training Partners/ Use the Buddy System

President Franklin Delano Roosevelt said, "People acting together as a group can accomplish things which no individual acting alone could ever hope to bring about."

Just as most students need a study buddy, athletes can benefit from a training partner who can push and challenge them at practice and before competitions. In fact, research has shown that when a peer teaches another athlete, they learn at a faster rate than when instructed under normal coach/athlete circumstances. The training partner could be a personal trainer, an athlete in another sport in the school, or even an older sibling, but most often a dedicated teammate can perform this duty.

The training partner and the athlete can work together to improve their physical stamina and mental outlooks because most likely on any given day, one of them will have a higher level of motivation. The point is that they eventually can come to count on each other for encouragement and support. Sports psychologist Jim Taylor, Ph.D., tells athletes, "The best person to have is a regular training partner, someone at about your level of ability and with similar goals. You can work together to accomplish your goals. The chances are on any given day that one of you will be motivated. Even if you're not very psyched to practice on a particular day, you will still put in the time and effort because your partner is counting on you."

Athletes can benefit from a training partner who can push and challenge them at practice and before competitions.

sirtravelalot/Shutterstock.com

The coach can assign the training partners (hopefully, athletes who have similar goals and motivation) or allow athletes to select their own partners. While establishing training partners works best in individual sports, like track and wrestling, it is certainly adaptable to all sports.

Having athletes work with a partner on a daily basis can contribute equally to athletes psychological and physical development. Their motivation and self-discipline improve when they are responsible to a specific teammate. Furthermore, their anxiety is often lessened when burdens can be shared with a partner. If they are paired correctly, each player shares the same goals and objectives as their counterpart, which can enhance their mental preparation for upcoming competitions.

Before you pair up members of your team, you should review their attitudes and goals. Partners must be mutually supportive—encouraging each other's improvement, enhancing each other's skills, and maximizing each other's conditioning. If each athlete views their partner's training as important as their own, then both typically perform better both in practice and in competition. Furthermore, both are more likely to recover from poor performances more quickly.

One type of buddy system is to have more mature senior athletes act as mentors for younger ones. Another is to link freshmen with freshmen, sophomores with sophomores, etc. Similar to utilizing mentors, the second option tends to match up players who know each other better and might, in fact, be friends outside the team. Either way gives athletes a sense of responsibility to themselves and their teammate; plus, they feel motivated to live up to their counterpart's expectations.

Drill partners should know to give minimum resistance at the beginning stages of drilling a technique and increased resistance through the repeated execution of that skill. This enables both athletes to gain confidence in mastering the technique and in each other. And by the first competition, the intent is for the athletes to feel responsible for the team's success and to support each other.

The results of this approach can be rewarding. Once coaches learn to share responsibility and become partners with their athletes, the kids take more pride in team success and have more at stake in team achievement. This method of coaching places more trust in the athletes, which has a positive effect on their self-esteem and motivation.

3

Midseason

Joseph Sohm/Shutterstock.com

Involve Alumni

Former players, if given enough notice, often love to return to the school and teach younger athletes the techniques and tactics that helped them become successful. Utilize them! Their participation as instructors can enhance practices and motivate your current players to master especially difficult techniques and skills.

Along with teaching technique, alumni can speak to current athletes at practices or even before a competition. Their personal anecdotes, recollections, and advice can be especially motivating, since current players will be hearing insights about competition from someone speaking in terms of their perspectives (i.e., they can truly relate to each other). You'd be wise, however, to caution alumni not to use profanity or to denigrate an opponent. Instead, ask them to comment on honoring traditions, working hard, and achieving success.

Alumni are crucial to your program. They are the salesmen for it in your absence, and they can make strong impressions on younger athletes. Their presence is truly invaluable. Former sports broadcaster Chris Schenkel states, "If you can turn one athlete into a little kid's hero, you might keep the kid from doing something he shouldn't do later."

Olena Yakobchuk/Shutterstock.com

Former players, if given enough notice, often love to return to the school and teach younger athletes the techniques and tactics that helped them become successful.

23 Involve Teachers

Positive and productive relationships with teachers can have a tremendous impact on an athlete's motivation. You develop this type of relationship by showing that you are concerned about the players' academics and behavior in school. Invite teachers to the competitions and solicit their advice, if needed, on dealing with certain athletes in the program. In short, involve them by inviting them to contribute to your program through one of the ways listed below.

Successful public relations for any athletic program begins in the school itself. Gaining the support of the faculty for the team should be given the highest priority. To turn teachers into advocates of your program there are a number of things you can do, including the following:

- Talk to them about the athletes and keep them informed about the team's progress. If they are anti-athletic, address it. Gain support by monitoring the athletes' academic standing in their classes and directing them to tutors, if needed.
- Invite the teachers to attend competitions. Offer them free passes, if necessary, and thank them afterwards for attending. You might even invite popular teachers to speak to the athletes before a practice or game.
- Convince them of their importance to your program. For example, you can initiate an "Adopt-a-Athlete" program where a faculty member can become the personal "cheerleader" for an athlete on the team (writing them notes, wishing them luck, inquiring about the games, etc).
- Seek their advice when you confront a problem with an athlete who has previously expressed respect for that teacher. You might even request that this faculty member join a conference you might have with that athlete.
- Give each faculty member a free media guide and send each one a copy of your newsletter.
- Invite the physical education teacher to put the team through an aerobic workout at the beginning of a practice early in the week.

Positive and productive relationships with teachers can have a tremendous impact on an athlete's motivation.

3DDock/Shutterstock.com

- Have the home economics teacher or school dietitian design a nutritional menu for your athletes.
- Have teachers complete an academic progress report each week for athletes who might be experiencing grade or eligibility problems in their classes. See Form 23-1 and 23-2.
- Ask the advisor to the school newspaper to have student reporters write articles about selected players.
- Give each teacher a copy of your schedule and goals at the beginning of the season and ask that they spend a moment between classes to encourage any athlete to achieve success in their games and in accomplishing their goals.
- Ask them to post a copy of the schedule in their classrooms and remind all students about upcoming competitions.
- Give all teachers a copy of your award winners at the end of the season so that they can congratulate them too.

MEMORANDUM
Academic Progress Report to Be Completed by Faculty

Name _____

Sport _____ Date _____

Directions: Each athlete is required to request the current grade/academic progress in their classes. Please indicate this below and include your signature. For borderline grades, indicate the lower grade. Thank you.

Course Name	Current Grade	Comments	Signature
Algebra 1	*C-*	*low quiz scores*	
1._____	_____	_____	_____
2._____	_____	_____	_____
3._____	_____	_____	_____
4._____	_____	_____	_____
5._____	_____	_____	_____
6._____	_____	_____	_____

Figure 23-1. An example of an athletic department form

MEMORANDUM
Academic Progress Report to Be Completed by Faculty

Student's Name _____

Subject _____ Date _____

Please rate as satisfactory (s) or unsatisfactory (u) this student in the following categories.
Return this form to coach _____ each Friday. Thank you!

S/U	Item	Comments
1._____	Attitude	_____
2._____	Homework	_____
3._____	Tests/quizzes	_____
4._____	Attendance	_____
5._____	Projects	_____
6._____	Current Grade	_____ Percent _____

Figure 23-2. Example of an athletic department academic progress report form

Involve Other Coaches **24**

You don't have to motivate your athletes alone. Your coaching colleagues would probably be honored to speak to your players and encourage them before competitions. Keep in mind that these athletes may also compete on their teams. Before you request any other coach to speak, discuss this with your coaching staff and plan accordingly (e.g., who, when, where, and what). The "what" refers to the topic; some possibilities in this regard include goal-setting, working hard, and overcoming failure (persistence).

You can even invite *opposing* coaches to talk to your players, typically directly after a competition. In this instance, opposing coaches could comment on the effort your players exhibited or the team's progress to that point in the season. At a minimum, be sure to tell your athletes about the praise the team receives from opposing coaches, when those coaches only express those compliments to you. Most athletes are inspired when they hear they have made a positive impression on adult coaches outside their own program. Once again, you should arrange this ahead of time and thank the other coach officially in a follow-up letter.

Joseph Sohm/Shutterstock.com

Coaches can even invite opposing *coaches to talk to their players.*

25 Involve Celebrities

Asking a local celebrity to speak to the team can bring media attention to your program, as well as motivate your athletes. A local celebrity could be an actor, performer, politician, or professional athlete, among others. In short, a celebrity is anyone who has achieved some level of fame or media attention. In my local community, we have a local television newscaster, a former football All-American, the mayor, and a best-selling author. All are educated, articulate, and positive; moreover, they enjoy speaking to the athletes about setting goals, keeping a positive attitude, and being successful.

Be cautious and selective about using professional athletes, however, to help motivate your players. Their reasons for competing (money, fame) can certainly differ from your athletes, so ask only the most appropriate professionals to speak to your team. It is very important to hear the content of their talk ahead of time and request that they do not speak off the cuff. The right pro athlete can have an enormous impact on the players and truly motivate them to drive to be successful.

Asking a local celebrity to speak to the team can bring media attention to a program, as well as motivate the athletes.

Natasa Adzic/Shutterstock.com

Involve Local Politicians

A fact of life is most politicians only gain office through elections, and a major way for them to communicate to the voting public is through the schools. Therefore, asking local politicians to support and praise the team in public is a win-win situation for both you and them. Moreover, your athletes can be both impressed and motivated when the mayor or a congressperson encourages them directly and personally in a speech or by letter at any point in their season. The city council could also compose official proclamations which commend the team or any individual member. Such formal documents may involve the term "whereas" repeatedly, but most kids will get the point—that the members of the government are impressed with their performances and want to acknowledge their importance to the community.

Niyazz/Shutterstock.com

Asking local politicians to support and praise the team in public is a win-win situation for both the team and the politicians.

27 Involve Cheerleaders/Spirit Club

Cheerleaders can be major source of motivation for athletes, regardless of their gender. Cheerleaders also include spirit groups, pep clubs, statisticians, and possibly the student council. These groups could contribute in a variety of ways. They can:

- Make posters and displays in school hallways.
- Organize pep assemblies and lead cheers.
- Advertise your program in the school.
- Increase the attendance at your games and tournaments.
- Photograph your players and highlight them in school display cases.
- Put a team schedule and pictures in community businesses and stores.
- Encourage other students to attend competitions.
- Send good luck notes to the athletes.

It is important to get the student body on your side, because with their support, the team can become even more inspired to be successful.

Once you get the cheerleaders or Pep Club involved, your guidance should be minimal, as long as each group's advisor is willing to participate in supporting your team. Attend one of their meetings, talk about your sport, and answer any questions. Then let them create their own cheers, signs, and banners. They might also provide beverages, snacks, or other treats after a game for the athletes.

Later, be sure to publicly acknowledge and thank them for their efforts.

sirtravelalot/Shutterstock.com

Cheerleaders can be major source of motivation for athletes, regardless of their gender.

Involve Administrators

Consider your position as a player on the school team and the administration as the coaching staff. Once you show support for the administration's policies, they in turn can become quite enthusiastic about supporting your program and your athletes. Although many administrators are burdened by the difficulties of supervising hundreds of other teachers and students combined, keep your athletic director, principal, and superintendent informed about your plans and all events related to your program, both good and bad.

To motivate players, invite administrators to speak to them at practices or possibly before a game. Ask administrators to assist with fundraising, pep assemblies, special uniform or transportation requests, and p.a. announcements. If they're unfamiliar with your sport, teach them the strategies and the scoring. Help them understand the sport's excitement and benefits. In short, seek their assistance in motivating your athletes.

Dragon_Fly/Shutterstock.com

To motivate players, invite administrators to speak to them at practices or possibly before a game.

29 Involve Civic Organizations

Too many coaches neglect school and civic organizations, which themselves are seeking ways to get involved in the school and help (and motivate) students. These groups of adults can support your program and serve indirectly to motivate athletes. The first step is to contact them and seek their support.

Potential support groups in the community are the Booster Club, Kiwanis, Rotary, American Legion, Lions, Chamber of Commerce, and local churches. By obtaining the support of these groups, your program may enjoy the financial and political support that most successful programs need to prosper. Begin by writing a letter to the organization's president where you introduce yourself and your program—a brief history and current expectations. Explain in your letter how you may want them to contribute to the team—attending games, making a donation, hosting a special event (an all-star wrestling match, for example), or purchasing some supplies. You should also request the opportunity to speak at their next meeting. A brief, enthusiastic speech can not only acquaint them with the team, it can also intensify their interest in your program. Maintain a connection and update them by sending them your media guide, newsletter, and schedule and returning to their meetings to speak.

Too many coaches neglect school and civic organizations, which themselves are seeking ways to get involved in the school and help (and motivate) students.

And don't neglect your own school board. Go to their meetings to announce updates about the team and to acknowledge specific players publicly. Later, have your players write thank you letters to specific individuals in the organization (see Figure 29-1).

This connection to the community can do much for you, your program, and your players. When they know they have the total support of adults outside their families, most athletes are both appreciative and inspired.

Dear Mr. _____ ,

The _____ High School _____ team is indeed grateful to you for your support of our program. Your generous donation of much needed funds enabled us to purchase Gatorade for use during our tournaments and after our games.

The coaches and players truly appreciate your interest and generosity. It is wonderful to recognize that there are community members like yourself interested in seeing our program succeed. We will certainly commit ourselves to fulfilling the expectations the community has for our program.

Once again, thank you for your dedicated effort directed toward our program. It is exciting to see community members support our players so enthusiastically. We hope to see you attend one or all of our competitions (a schedule is enclosed) and thank you personally.

Gratefully,

The Coaching Staff and Players of _____ High School

Figure 29-1. An example of a thank you letter to a community member

30 Involve Parents

Parents can be your most important support group. Indeed, you should establish a nucleus of support for your program from parents who understand and respect your coaching philosophy. "I'd non-renew a coach if he or she had a communication problem with parents, students, or administrators," says Joe Webb, a former principal at Mentor (OH) High School. "A coach has to get all these people to believe in his program."

To motivate athletes, it is mandatory that you form a positive relationship with their parents. You gain parental support by being available to discuss the athlete's progress, providing technical information about the sport in simpler terms, and regularly informing them (use a newsletter) about any policies, events, or updates related to the team. You lessen parents' questions and concerns by providing written information (see Figure 30-1) where these matters are answered. One avenue for distributing this important information is at the "Meet the Team" night.

What can parents do for you? They can make phone calls, write letters, send emails, or talk personally to athletes who may need more motivation. They can be sure their child is getting the proper nutrition and rest. And they can attend competitions, cheer for the team, and generally support the program.

Just be careful, warns Jack Lesyk, Ph.D., who is a sport psychologist, of parents who don't know how to support the team effectively. "Sometimes adults project their own unfulfilled dreams, motivations, and goals onto their children."

Such difficulties can often be eliminated through open and candid dialogues with parents. Lesyk recommends that the coach explain to parents how to talk to their son or daughter about their feelings about competitions. The coach, according to Lesyk, needs to teach parents to teach their children how "to define success in terms of their attainment of their own goals" and "downplay winning and external rewards." Clearly, both the coach and parent(s) have the same objective: a motivated athlete who is excited about competing and attentive to coaching.

CONGRATULATIONS!

_____ (insert name of athlete) has made an important commitment in regards to their decision to join the high school _____ (insert your sport name team). The coaching staff is very pleased to have _____ (insert athlete's name) as a member of the program, and we have organized our efforts to promote their individual success.
_____ (insert your sport name) is a very demanding sport and requires much effort and dedication from all athletes. We admire and respect _____ (insert name of athlete) already for making this type of commitment.

OUR SEASON

The season officially begins on _____ (date) and continues through _____ (date). This means, of course, we will have practices each school day and on Saturdays. Practices run from 2:45 PM to 5:15 PM (showers follow). Our competitions begin in _____ (date). I have enclosed a copy of our schedule.

PRE-SEASON INFORMATION

I expect all potential players to engage themselves in a conditioning program at the school every Monday, Wednesday, and Friday after school from 2:45-4:15 PM. They will weightlift, do agility drills and flexibility exercises, and run.

FORMS

Participation in _____ (insert name of sport) also involves some important forms for both the athlete and parents to complete. I have enclosed them in this envelope. Please have _____ (insert name of athlete) return them to me as soon as possible.

THANK YOU

The coaches certainly appreciate your support in encouraging _____ (insert name of athlete) to compete. This is a big challenge, and we know that He could experience some difficulties during the season. But if we work together, your son/daughter's season can be very rewarding.

Finally, we also look forward to seeing you at our games. Parents can also order sweaters that display our school colors and name. An order form is enclosed.

Sincerely,

Figure 30-1. An example of a letter to parents

4

All Season

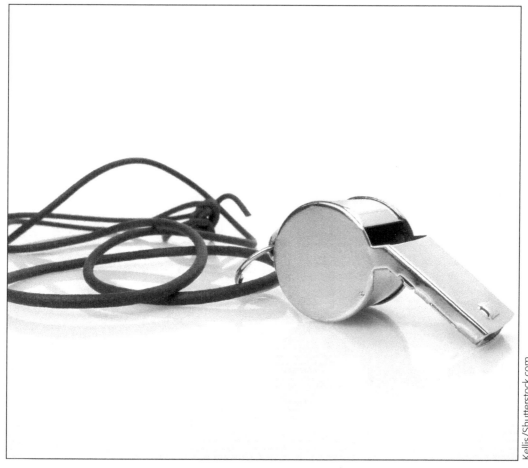

Kellis/Shutterstock.com

Communicate **31**

Clearly, good coaching requires good communication. Coaches need to consider how they transmit messages and how athletes interpret them. The following are examples of things that can get in the way of effective communication and, in turn, effective motivation:

- Poor verbal skills by the coach
- Athletes who don't pay attention
- Athletes who don't understand verbal cues
- Messages that are inconsistent
- An environment that threatens open dialogue

Unfortunately, most instances of communication occur when coaches tell their athletes what they're doing *wrong*. In fact, these instances are often characterized by statements like, "C'mon, try again. Do it right," "What's wrong with you?," "That's not how to do it," or "C'mon, *think*."

Instead, coaches would get better results if they provided exact information about the correct technique or behavior as in "Be sure you push off the starting block" instead of "You gotta get outa there faster!" They should be more concerned with teaching than judging, especially with those athletes who may already have low self-esteem.

Good coaching requires good communication.

muzsy/Shutterstock.com

When athletes hear judgmental language, they often become tense and uneasy, even defensive, certainly less motivated. Any worries they may have had about achieving their goals become magnified.

The degree of motivation may vary from athlete to athlete, but each individual is entitled to the same acceptance, respect, and concern, and the coach's complete attention when they communicate. Most often, the better the coach communicates, the more motivated the athletes will be.

Allow players to communicate as well. Greg Shelley of the Janssen Sports Leadership Center, which is affiliated with the Champion Coaches Network, advises coaches "to check with [their] athletes to determine if what [they] are communicating to them is understood, what they need, and what they want. Encourage your leaders to make suggestions as to how things (e.g., practices, travel, game day preparations, etc.) might be improved. Remember, if you are asking for input, at least be willing to incorporate something (a suggestion) at some point." Coaches can invite their athletes to provide input into any plans for the program and then discuss the contribution they want to make. Here, you are both setting up open communication and fostering their commitment.

This approach is echoed by Sara Robinson, MA: "When athletes feel as if they have a say, or some control within a situation, motivation can increase. *What can you do?* Consider giving options within training: Do they want to start with Drill A or Drill B? Would they like to condition on Monday or Wednesday of next week? You can still retain a lot of control while giving athletes some of the say, which will likely enhance the motivation of the team members."

Whether your means of communication is accomplished mainly by personal conferences or team discussions (and you should do both!), the athletes need to see that you are articulate, concerned, and specific when you talk. You show that you are articulate when you choose your words carefully. You demonstrate concern when you speak more about their health, family, and academics than on their athletic performances. Finally, athletes understand you better when your comments are specific and direct.

Listen 32

Effective motivation clearly stems from effective communication, but communication must be more than just the coach talking. You also have to listen to the athletes and comprehend what they're saying. The athlete needs to see communication as a mutual, two-way process. When communicating, you must especially be an effective listener. This means you are accessible to listening and giving adequate time to hear what the athlete wants to say.

As the athlete talks, you should focus intensely on what they say and repeat the message as you understand it to see if your understanding is correct. Also, never interrupt the athlete. For example, an appropriate response could be "What I hear you saying is . . ." followed by your exact recollection of the athlete's comments. Regardless of what they say, hold back any emotional or judgmental response.

This is termed active listening, as opposed to passive, silent listening. In active listening, you interact with the athlete by providing them with a paraphrased response that proves you understand what they have said. Dr. Alan Goldberg adds, "The way to make an athlete feel better about themselves is to listen to them when they speak to you and to attempt to understand them from their perspective. Be silent when they talk, don't plan your next comment and try to step into their shoes. Your efforts will pay off in a strong relationship and a motivated athlete."

And don't neglect those physical mannerisms that make up non-verbal communication: head and hand movements, gestures, touching, body position, even the tone of your voice are all associated with any act of verbal communication.

In summary, effective listening involves:
1. Being accessible to listening by giving adequate time to hear what the athlete wants to say.
2. Focusing intensely on what the athlete says.
3. Repeating the message as you understand it to see if your understanding is correct, for example, "What I hear you saying is . . ."
4. Not interrupting the athlete.
5. Not responding emotionally.
6. Seeking clarification for any comments you do not understand.

33 Respect All Players on the Team

"Deal with your athletes the way that you would like to be dealt with," says Dr. Alan Goldberg. "Respect them and they will respect you, be able to learn from you, and will go to the ends of the earth to perform for you." In short, each athlete, regardless of their talent, ability, or skills, whether they routinely struggle in competitions or often achieve victory, deserves the coach's total respect.

An old saying is, to get respect you have to give respect. The intent of this segment is not to debate that statement; instead, this point simply advocates the importance of respecting each athlete's personal motivations and abilities. A more appropriate statement might be, to motivate athletes you have to respect them.

Would *you* work hard for a coach if you did not feel they respected you? Probably not. That said, use the term *respect* when you dialogue with your athletes and be sure they understand what it means.

Especially consider the athletes who are junior varsity or on second or third teams. They are as important to any program as the superstars. Certainly, they have to learn to "pay their dues," but they should be treated with as much attention and respect as the varsity.

Furthermore, no athlete deserves a mediocre level of attention from the coach. Therefore, spend some time with each athlete during practices and/or the school day and develop a system involving the entire coaching staff. The coaches must acknowledge each player each day (for instance, if there are four coaches and forty players, each coach makes sure to have some contact with 10 players each day). And if an athlete needs to talk, make time. When athletes recognize that the events in their lives and their concerns matter to you and that you respect them, you increase their level of motivation in your sport.

Show Fairness 34

Along with respect, fairness is a very important trait for a coach to have. All athletes, even professionals, want to know their coaches are being fair with them. Athletes' motivation lessens if they feel the coach's decisions are either arbitrary or self-serving. The first step to showing fairness is establishing the standards by which the team is to operate, and the second step is to follow them.

Sara Robinson, MA, summarizes, "Your team is made up of individuals, and a person can be motivated by many different factors which may change day-to-day, or moment-to-moment, making motivation a complex and dynamic process." To maintain this "dynamic process" and to keep an effective balance between all members of the team, the coach has to treat all of them fairly.

Fairness is often an emotional issue for athletes. According to Dominique Stasulli in the article "How Coaches Contribute to Athletes' Motivation," "In many ways, the coach plays a pivotal nurturing role by responding to an athlete's emotional and physical needs. The surrounding climate dictated by the coach, whether it's critical or motivational, affects the athlete's psychosocial well-being." In other words, coaches have to be especially attentive to how they treat the players on their team.

Don't grant some athletes time off, for example, if you refuse the same request from others. Don't give some athletes special privileges unless *all* athletes have the opportunity to earn them. And don't highlight or praise the same players repeatedly. In each case, it may seem you are doing something positive for your athletes, but in actuality you are showing a lack of fairness.

Greg Shelley of the Janssen Sports Leadership Center, writes "Give your athletes a reason to want to work hard—take the time to develop genuine, honest, caring, and trusting relationships with your players. Athletes will work harder (and longer) for someone they know genuinely believes in them, cares about them, and is committed to helping them achieve their potential. At the heart of player motivation . . . is the quality of the coach-athlete relationship." In short, treat your athletes consistently and fairly.

35 Promote Academics

One athlete says, "I'm motivated when I know that the coach is concerned about me as an athlete *and* as a student. He has to be straightforward with you and not feed you some line. He has to look out for you but not pamper you. When I came out of middle school, I was the top dog and I kind of had a big head. My coach set me straight and got me going in the right direction. He also let me know that there was more to life than football."

Karol Stewart, whose son competed on the varsity golf and wrestling teams in high school, says, "I think the coaches should help him build his skills, but they better keep his training and studies in a proper perspective. I think the coaches should reaffirm what his father and I have been trying to tell him all along about his academics."

"A coach has to model a strong work ethic," says one former Ohio middle school principal, "and he has to promote scholarship in the classroom."

Clearly, if coaches want motivated athletes, they must support the athlete's academic obligations and even assist them with any of their subjects if they can. The athletes, their parents, and your administrators all need to know that you are concerned about each athlete's academic standing. Dr. Alan Goldberg states, "Take an interest in your athlete beyond their athletic abilities. If you care about them as a person rather than just what they can do for the team, they will reward you with high motivation, increased intensity and great performances."

Chinnapong/Shutterstock.com

If coaches want motivated athletes, they must support the athlete's academic obligations and even assist them with any of their subjects if they can.

We all recognize that the athlete's performance in the classroom is much more important than their results in competitions, especially when eligibility is considered. Therefore, you should be especially attentive to each player's academic standing—assisting those with tutoring or time off who are having difficulties and rewarding those who are earning high grades. They will be motivated by such efforts.

You might also consider setting up a "study table," where athletes gather before practice to complete homework or review for tests. A weekly or bi-weekly progress report could be arranged for any athlete you believe is doing poorly in the classroom. If problems (low grades, missing assignments, poor test results) do occur, you can respond to them promptly with a tutoring session or time off from practice.

It is gratifying to note the comments of superstar professional athletes on the importance of academics:

- "I was always academically oriented. It was a matter of pride and self-esteem. I wanted to be able to hold my own." (Lou Brock, former Major League Baseball outfielder)
- "The single most important goal for a student-athlete . . . should be to achieve a good education . . . Without an education, it will be impossible to meet the challenge of our ever-changing world." (Alan Page, former National Football League defensive tackle and later a Minnesota judge)
- "Education is the most important part of your school days. Therefore, you should concentrate on this and recognize that athletics are only a part of your life and should be played as such. You should realize that athletics are still [just] sports to be enjoyed." (Pancho Gonzales, former professional tennis player)
- "It is of prime importance, therefore, that academics or schoolwork be given great emphasis. The years of high school and college are great learning years which can result in big payoffs and much happiness. This concentration on academics can only make you a better athlete." (John MacLeod, former National Basketball Association head coach)

36 Up the Ante

Athletes get motivated when the coaching staff challenges them to learn new techniques, attempt new agility skills, or practice harder than the day before. New challenges are great motivators. According to Anne Josephson, "Making things too easy actually decreases [athletes'] motivation. Having high expectations and assignments that are challenging but attainable with reasonable effort is the motivational sweet spot."

Improvement and accomplishment are two keys to this method of motivation. First, athletes must see each practice as a challenge to improve their skills and, second, as another step toward being successful in actual competitions. They should sense, for instance, by the end of each practice that they have met that day's challenge and taken another step towards achieving their personal goals. They should feel more confident and motivated for the next practice session, after their work that day has been completed.

Athletes reach their potential faster when they are challenged by the coaches, when they are pushed by their drill partner, or when their abilities are stretched at practice each day. In some respects, each practice is itself a competition. Practices should be designed, therefore, to test the athletes' physical and mental skills, while allowing for mistakes, corrections, improvement, and finally success. If your practice accomplishes this, then your athletes will stay motivated.

Athletes reach their potential faster when they are challenged by the coaches, when they are pushed by their drill partner, or when their abilities are stretched at practice each day.

"I'm motivated when I'm pushed beyond my limits," says one varsity athlete. "I like competing, because it brings out the best in everyone. My coaches have encouraged me to strive to be the best."

Motivation in pressure situations also needs to be addressed. Preparing for any competition is seldom fun for athletes because it normally involves extensive physical and mental effort. Plus, the failure to master new techniques or skills can be both demoralizing and debilitating to an athlete. Dr. Alan Goldberg's advice? "Teach your athletes that failures and setbacks are a necessary part of the learning process and not a cause for embarrassment or quitting. Model this attitude and you'll motivate your athletes to take risks and really go for it. If you jump in an athlete's face whenever he messes up, you'll demotivate him and get him worrying about failing."

Coaches should also make practice more appealing by placing the athletes in situations that lead to them being successful and build their confidence. According to Michael Reinboth and Joan Duda, writing in *The Sport Psychologist*, in a climate where mastering a variety of skills is essential, an athlete's "self-esteem can be built up gradually" when coaches comment more often on the athlete's improvement and "work ethic." If coaches emphasize "the process" more than "immediate outcomes," athletes stay motivated despite their initial failures.

In this instance, motivation and a potential competitor can become linked. Dr. Jim Taylor, a sports psychologist, often tells athletes, "Another way to keep yourself motivated is to focus on your greatest competitor. Identify who your biggest competition is and put his or her name or photo where you can see it every day. Ask yourself, 'Am I working as hard as him/her?' Remember that only by working your hardest will you have a chance to overcome your greatest competitor." Using this technique definitely can help up the ante for some athletes.

You can capitalize on the athletes' intrinsic motivation by challenging them to learn new techniques, but remember to tolerate their errors because they are natural to any learning process. Your personal expectations for each athlete also have much to do with their level of motivation and maturation. Certainly, challenge them but have reasonable expectations of them as well.

37 Set Daily Goals

Typically, whenever goals are addressed in athletics, most individuals associate them with winning games. However, *daily* goals should be about mastering certain techniques or performing specific skills—what researcher Andrew Hamilton terms to be "predominantly process-oriented" objectives. That said, express these goals in simple terms, and then the coaching staff must do their best to enable *all* players to master that technique or skill. Athletes are usually motivated by any form of accomplishment, even if it is mastering the correct way to step on a blocking drill or sinking 10 free throws in a row.

Announce the goal at the beginning of the practice or the competition. For example: "Today everyone has to show he can hit a curveball. Our pitchers are only going to throw curveballs, and I'm confident that within the hour you all will be able to hit one for a base hit." Or: "We are going to end this scrimmage today without a single penalty called against us. No offsides, no illegal blocks, no illegal motion—we will not see a single yellow flag dropped because of something we did."

Each practice must have a goal, an objective the coaching staff mandates beforehand that the team has to accomplish. That goal has to be addressed with the team at the beginning of practice. Hopefully, by the end of practice, that goal should be achieved. Former Iowa University wrestling coach Dan Gable, whose Hawkeye teams won 15 NCAA Division I national championships, recommends that in "every practice session you need to emphasize the areas that give you trouble and drill in those areas. It is important that you feel some self-satisfaction after every practice." Anne Josephson adds, "When [an athlete] does not understand the next step or what is going to happen, it is demotivating. Clear goals are motivating."

Avoid, however, announcing too many daily goals—one to three is enough per day. If you have too many and fail to accomplish one or two, then frustration can set in and lessen the athletes' motivation. Achieving even a single goal, however, can build confidence and, in turn, motivation.

Finally, a coach can use the approach that Dr. Jim Taylor employs with athletes when he presents them with "two questions. When you get up in the morning, ask, 'What can I do today to become the best athlete I can be?' And before you go to sleep, ask, 'Did I do everything possible today to become the best athlete I can be?' These two questions will remind [the athlete] daily of what [their] goals are and will challenge [them] to be motivated to do [their] best."

Set Weekly Goals

Athletes, when informed of the goal(s) for the week, feel both a sense of direction and purpose. They will be especially motivated if, in fact, they can participate in creating the goal(s). You could, for instance, ask after Saturday's game or at the beginning of Monday's practice what they feel the team needs to work on. Maybe, they're disappointed by their field goal percentage or their times in the last track meet. If so, ask them to state purposeful goals for the week (e.g., "increase our field goal percentage by 20%" or "reduce our relay times by at least 10 seconds overall" or "earn 10 more takedowns in our next wrestling match").

Be sure that these goals are stated in specific terms (not "let's shoot better" or "we need to get in better shape"), that they are measurable, and that they are achievable. Athletes are first motivated when they are reminded each day of the weekly goals and again if they achieve them. Moreover, "[g]oals need to be monitored and revised on a regular basis," asserts Andrew Hamilton. "One of the biggest mistakes that coaches make in setting goals is that they are often too rigid in their approach. The goal-setting process works best, when there is some flexibility and the individual athlete or team take ownership of each goal."

Dr. Jim Taylor, referencing the *grind* of the season, reveals that when confronted with the exhaustion and tension associated with athletics, too many younger athletes "are not likely to stay motivated." He advises coaches to acknowledge the physical drudgery and mental challenges that take place on a weekly basis and to tell their athletes that they should "neither love nor hate the *grind*; [they should] just accept it as part of the deal in striving toward [their] goals. The *grind* may not be very enjoyable, but what does feel good is seeing . . . hard work pay off with success."

Athletes, when informed of the goal(s) for the week, feel both a sense of direction and purpose.

patpitchaya/Shutterstock.com

39 Set Seasonal Goals

Ladd Holman, a former head wrestling coach at Delta (UT) High School, whose teams won 23 state titles, had a simple formula for success that involved following a sequence of steps: set a specific goal for the season; decide what needs to be sacrificed to reach the goal; and then work hard enough to achieve the goal.

Sports psychologist Jim Taylor, Ph.D., when addressing younger athletes, often comments, "There are few things more rewarding and motivating than setting a goal, putting effort toward the goal, and achieving the goal. The sense of accomplishment and validation of the effort makes you feel good and motivates you to strive higher. It's valuable to establish clear goals of what you want to accomplish in your sport and how you will achieve those goals. Seeing that your hard work leads to progress and results should motivate you further to realize your goals.

"When I speak to groups of young athletes, I always ask how many have big goals, like going to the Olympics or playing pro ball. About 90 percent raise their hands. I then ask how many are doing everything they can to achieve their goals. Only one or two tentative hands go up. What this tells me is that there is often a big gap between the goals athletes have and the effort they are putting into those goals. It's easy to say that you want to be a successful athlete. It is much more difficult to actually make it happen. If you have this kind of disconnect, you have two choices. You can either lower goals to match your effort or you can raise your effort to match your goals."

Like the coming attractions for a movie, a seasonal goal is something the athletes see and enjoy later, specifically by the end of the season. If designed correctly, seasonal goals keep the entire team on the same path and headed in the same direction. Often, these are phrased in terms like "win the league," "make it to the state playoffs," or "go undefeated," but these seasonal goals could have nothing to do with winning. They could, for instance, promote team camaraderie (no one quits), academics (everyone has a 2.5 GPA or better), or rules (no one breaks training rules).

Initially seasonal goals, need to be created by the team as a whole. In this instance, Andrew Hamilton says, "[C]oaches and managers are better off exercising some democracy when setting goals, particularly if working with more experienced athletes." Second, they should focus on what the athletes should *do*. Finally, they should be phrased in terms of positive outcomes. For example, the first goals of the following is phrased incorrectly, while the second expresses the same goal in a more positive way:
- We will not commit any penalties against ____ High School.
- We will play a penalty-free match against ____ High School.

Again, phrase goals in terms of what you want the athletes to do. For example, a team goal may be to decrease by fifteen percent the relay times by the end of the season or to increase the total amount of poundage on the bench press. Avoid goals like "dominate our opponents" or "do our best," which are often vague and unmeasurable.

This approach for "developing a strong sense of *purpose* is most effective for promoting long-term motivation," says Greg Shelley, writing for the Champion Coaches Network. "Creating a sense of purpose and/or meaning is about changing the way athletes think about their roles, their reasons for coming to practice, their influence on teammates, their membership on the team, and their reasons for playing and competing. Providing purpose and meaning is about creating an environment that is conducive to personal growth and encouraging athletes to motivate themselves, as well as inspire their teammates. Developing purpose and meaning takes more time and energy (investment), but it can lead to that long-term motivation for which most coaches are striving."

The competitions in the early season could be considered simply as training sessions, as valuable learning experiences, or as steppingstones to the state-sponsored tournaments or playoff games at the end of the season. Unfortunately, too many coaches feel threatened by early season losses. Similarly, too many athletes see them as indicators of their entire season. The more important goals reflect what the individual athletes and the coaching staff want to accomplish by the *end* of the season. Everything before that should be seen as competitive training sessions that offer valuable experiences.

Emphasize to athletes the importance of establishing seasonal goals and, of course, involve them in the formation of those goals. They need to see that goals are helpful, that they add a competitive challenge (motivation) for the squad and prompt a better work ethic. Examples of meaningful seasonal goals include the following:
- Prioritize the health of the athletes.
- Educate the athletes about the value of hard work, cooperation, self-discipline, and commitment.
- Promote an enjoyment of the sport.
- Empower athletes to set individual goals.
- Foster a desire to be successful.
- Demand that the school be represented in a respectful and dignified manner.
- Promote a successful relationship with parents, the community and the school administration.
- Encourage victory in competitions.

According to Andrew Hamilton, "Through empowering athletes to set their own goals, they are more likely to accept the challenges that lie ahead and pursue the goals with enthusiasm. To keep athletes on track with their long-term goals, they should also set appropriate medium-term goals. For example, following a bronze medal-winning performance at the 2004 Athens Olympics, UK heptathlete Kelly Sotherton set herself the medium-term goal of winning the 2006 Commonwealth title in Melbourne (which she achieved), en route to pursuing her long-term goal to be crowned Olympic champion at the 2008 Beijing Games."

The coaching staff should not set all the season goals alone. All members of the team must be involved. You could even talk to administrators and some parents and get their input. The group has to operate with one positive direction—e.g., "be league champions"—which should be clarified either at the beginning or end of every practice, until the goal has been accomplished. These goals must be sound, reasonable, and reachable.

Then, be sure that every athlete feels that they are making a strong contribution to achieving these goals. No one, including assistant coaches, should feel that they are only along for the ride, that their input or effort doesn't really count, that the superstars are the only ones helping the team be successful. Second- and third-teamers have to see that their effort is for a worthwhile purpose.

In short, seasonal goals are challenges. They are a means of making the coaches and the athletes' efforts purposeful. They are essential for any program. David Hemery analyzed the importance of goals established cooperatively between the coach and players in his book *The Pursuit of Sporting Excellence.* "The mutual effort towards a common goal," writes Hemery, "brings a closeness and sharing and this enhances communication. This makes the process valuable in itself, regardless of the outcome."

Before you can discuss goals with your athletes, you need to have a more private discussion. This one is with yourself. You need to discern the goals *you* want to accomplish— goals so important, in fact, that you will not procrastinate, relax, or quit until they are achieved. Maintain a positive attitude and a clear focus on those goals.

"Common goals, similar attitudes, mutual respect—that's what creates a successful season," says Rex Holman who won a national wrestling championship his senior year for Ohio State University. The same results can happen for your team if you set meaningful goals, develop an organized plan of action, and follow through with passion and diligence.

Coaches can adopt the approach Dr. Jim Taylor takes when he tells athletes, "[F]ocus on your long-term goals. Remind yourself why you're working so hard. Imagine exactly what you want to accomplish and tell yourself that the only way you'll be able to reach your goals is to continue to work hard. Try to generate feelings of inspiration and pride that you will experience when you reach your goals. This technique will distract you from the discomfort of the *grind*, focus you on what you want to achieve, and generate positive thoughts and emotions that will get you through the *grind*."

Avoid Pressurized Goals

A pressurized goal resembles a statement like "We *have* to win this one." This can work against motivation, not enhance it. Certainly, you may feel demanding a certain result (e.g., a winning season or a margin of victory by twenty points in the next game) is simply a means to challenge players, but most of them will see it as pressure, which prompts tension more often than triumph.

You need to stress improvement, not wins. If your goals surface from dialogues with all members of the team, then they are not likely to be pressurized goals. Instead, goals designed cooperatively between coaches and players are far more appealing and prompt much less anxiety. If you still remain uncertain if pressure is linked to any goal, talk to your administrators or to other coaches and get their feedback. If it is, then make an adjustment.

Dr. Alan Goldberg asserts that coaches lessen the pressure of goal-setting by creating "[c]learly defined goals." Coaches must then "work with [their] athletes at the beginning and throughout the season on specific, measurable, clearly define goals that they can break down into long-term, intermediate and short-term pieces. Help your athletes make sense of every practice in relation to their long-term goals."

The bricks that make up the foundation of the athletic program are your personal principles. These principles determine the decisions you make, the goals you and the team set, and the attitude you express each day. Keep your athletes motivated by never presenting a pressurized goal to your athletes; they probably already have enough to deal with.

Coaches need to stress improvement, not wins.

41 Have Fun

Howard Ferguson, legendary Ohio wrestling coach, whose St. Edward High School teams won 10 state titles, offered this caution to coaches: "The next time you're getting ready to play a game, ask yourself why you're playing. A game is not supposed to be work. It's not something you have to do . . . Do it for fun. Do it because you want to do it. Practice is the hard part; the game should be fun . . . Stop worrying about winning and losing. If you've prepared right, you shouldn't have to worry."

Former Olympic and Indiana University swim coach James "Doc" Counsilman used silly antics and obnoxious humor to make his swimming practices fun.

A varsity wrestler adds: "Practice has to be fun. I want practice to raise my level of competition, but I also expect the coach to give all athletes an equal chance and help all the athletes in the same way."

Joe Namath says, "When you have confidence, you can have a lot fun, and when you have fun, you can do amazing things."

Be sure, therefore, to add fun into the learning process. While repetition is needed in drills, learning need not be boring or dull. You could possibly, as an example, without saying a word, teach an entire practice using pantomime, charades, and gestures to make points and teach techniques. "Create an atmosphere of fun on your team, and

While repetition is needed in drills, learning need not be boring or dull.

you will motivate your athletes to train harder and longer," says Dr. Alan Goldberg. "If practice is nothing but uninterrupted drudgery, your athletes will quickly lose interest. If you really want your athletes to be serious competitors and come through in the clutch for you, regularly introduce humor and fun in practice."

Consider that an exhaustive practice doesn't necessarily translate into winning games. Concentrate on having fun, teaching the fundamentals, and building the self-esteem of the athletes. Your better athletes will always find a way to win, regardless of the amount of emphasis that is placed on victory, and your less-skilled athletes will find the sport to be rewarding. "Sometimes I find myself getting a little too serious," admits professional tennis player Andre Agassi. "When I'm having fun, it breaks the tension, and I play much better."

Fun could come from playing a game sometime during practice. You still need to design practices that begin with clear objectives and involve specific activities, but inserting a game (e.g., relay races for soccer players or knee football on the mat for wrestlers) can give a tremendous motivational boost to athletes. One baseball coach even had an Easter egg hunt out on the diamond that had players running around and scooping plastic eggshells with candy inside. The athletes were still active, but the rigor of practice was replaced, at least for a short period, by a fun activity. Once you play a game in practice, you will probably hear your players request that you do it again. Use that request as a motivator (e.g., if everyone accomplishes a certain task in a set time limit, you can let them play a game). Your players will tend to work their hardest for the opportunity to play that game.

Therefore, develop a sense of humor and try to organize drills in practice into fun and challenging competitions. A middle school football player admits, "I keep participating when the coach makes me feel good about myself, when he makes practice fun."

42 Use Data and Statistics

To some coaches, statistics are meaningless (with the exception of wins and losses). However, most athletes always seem to be interested in, for example, their tackles, their personal w/l record, or their times. That said, the coach should post statistical charts (related to the athlete's individual performance in recent competitions and over the season as a whole) that reveal clearly the athlete's progress towards achievement. Coaches should also post, of course, data related to the overall team's performance, like the team's total number of first downs, team free throw percentage, or average goals per game, for instance.

Display these statistics on a locker room bulletin board each week, possibly daily, during the season. Do this routinely, because athletes need constant feedback. They get motivated by seeing objective results of their efforts in practice, especially when the statistics show improvement. Statistics and data can identify for athletes their strengths and weaknesses in the sport and help them get self-directed to eliminate those weaknesses. For instance, a basketball player with a lower free throw percentage than field goal percentage can often be seen staying after practice shooting at the foul line. That happens because their observation of posted statistics has motivated them to correct a weak area of their game.

Classroom teachers use data-driven lessons. Likewise, data can be used in athletics to motivate athletes. For example, a coach can provide statistics related to the days, possibly the hours, the athletes have put into their training and preparation (Include time spent outside of practice as well). The total number could be impressive and, in turn, motivational. Use this data to demonstrate the connection between time spent at practice and success in competitions. This can encourage better practice attendance and show the importance of consistent effort to achieving both team and personal goals.

To be sure, to some coaches, statistics and data are less important than the relationships they have with their athletes. And unfortunately, on occasion, the data/stats can reveal a player's lack of success. In this instance, Dr. Alan Goldberg advises, "Let your athlete know that you are even more there for them when they have a bad performance than when they have a good one."

Nevertheless, most athletes always seem to be interested in statistics. That said, coaches should post statistical charts related to the athlete's individual performances in competitions over the season that reveal clearly their progress. In that regard, using data can be a productive motivator.

Be Honest

William Shakespeare's character Polonius in Hamlet says in Act I, "This above all: To thine own self, be true. And it must follow as the night the day, thou canst not be false to any man." Unlike Polonious, for many of us, being totally straightforward with athletes can be difficult. We may fear hurting a young person's feelings or lessening their self-esteem, but if we conceal the truth from players or mislead them, we may ruin our relationship and rapport with our athletes.

It becomes a matter of integrity. If you are sincere about teaching athletes to obey the rules and compete fairly, then you must do the same. You have to be honest with them. This topic is so significant that three major Ohio colleges have semester courses for students in ethics alone. Coaches, it seems, need training in how to be ethical and reflect honesty.

You may find it useful to address your concerns regularly throughout the season, even weekly. One varsity athlete respects his coach for speaking out. "He has also taught me how to overcome hardships," he claims, "how to take pride in the team, not to cheat ever. He's a strict coach."

If you want to be recognized for operating an honest program, you need to have strong ethics and character. The head coach, therefore, needs to instruct assistants why integrity is important. The public must see the staff as individuals who take responsibility for their actions and refuse to compromise their values, even when the issue is unpopular or winning is put in jeopardy.

A coach has to develop in their athletes a sense of pride in a program that functions by the rules.

Even if you are desperate to win, you cannot violate ethical behavior. Cheating cheapens the value of winning; true glory comes when victory is achieved honestly and fairly.

A coach has to develop in their athletes a sense of pride in a program that functions by the rules. This doesn't happen easily or quickly for most teenagers, who rarely find fault in ignoring an authority's rules. You should spend the time to explain the importance of integrity to them. This may be a conversation you repeat often.

Honest actions must be a part of your program consistently. "Truth has no special time of its own," says Albert Schweitzer, the French physician. "Its hour is now—always." Athletes need to believe in you, and they can usually tell when a coach isn't being honest or consistent. They get motivated by a coach who is always honest and ethical. Dominique Stasulli in her article "How Coaches Contribute to Athletes' Motivation," advises that "[c]oaches should strongly urge athletes to be smart about their competitive mindset and the damaging consequences of [dishonesty] . . . mental toughness is better measured with humble honesty rather than stubborn pride."

Finally, you need to carefully consider the incentives you provide to motivate your athletes. Their age, maturity level, interests, and culture are important in this instance. You must be a disciplined person. Regarding ethical behavior, you may be the only role model the athletes follow.

Encourage Them

For most athletes, encouragement must be continuous and constructive. Athletes feel encouraged when they realize you are dedicated toward their personal success and find multiple opportunities to commend their actions and achievements.

Coaches should, in fact, never base achievement on outcomes. You probably need to define achievement in as many ways as you have athletes. A coach who uses encouragement to motivate athletes rewards effort, not success; publicizes ability, not outcomes; and sees victory as the athletes' (or the team's), not the coach's. A coach like this uses encouragement, not anger, to motivate athletes.

Athletes can also encourage other athletes. The plan in this instance is to involve athletes who have found the sport to be so rewarding and enjoyable that they are eager to tell that to others. As their coach, though, be sure that your older athletes say the right things. For example, "I tell them that I play football because it's fun and exciting," says a varsity running back. "But you have to be ready to push yourself."

Most coaches agree that you don't win with the techniques you know; you win with the athletes you train. Clearly, the athlete's physical talent and personal commitment become crucial elements in both individual and team success. Therefore, coaches who spend time encouraging their athletes do much to increase their level of commitment, motivation, and ultimately team success.

Athletes can also encourage other athletes.

Brocreative/Shutterstock.com

45 Stress the Importance of Rest

Anne Josephson is succinct and direct on this issue: "An exhausted [athlete] will have a hard time staying motivated. Sleep is essential."

This sentiment is echoed by Dr. Alan Goldberg: "Rest is part of good training. If an athlete does not get a chance to rest, they will ultimately burn out, either mentally or physically. Short breaks in training over the course of the season will keep your athletes physically and mentally fresh and insure that they stay."

Coaches, therefore, should emphasize the importance of rest at the first team meeting, at the "Meet the Team" night for parent/guardians to hear, and weekly at the end of practice. If a player neglects to get 7-9 hours of sleep daily, they risk becoming exhausted too readily at practice or, at worst, physically ill. Obtaining proper rest is crucial for athletes who want to perform up to their potential. If they are well-rested, they will be more motivated at practices and in competitions.

Rest is part of good training.

Monkey Business Images/Shutterstock.com

Employ a Variety of Drills **46**

It is clear that today's coaches should employ far more sophisticated training methods than were needed just 10 years ago. If the skills of the sport can become instinctive for athletes, they can perform more successfully in a competition. Experienced coaches know to use repetition in practice so their players perform more by quick reflex than delayed reaction. Players then feel more confident about their abilities and more motivated to compete.

The problem is that repetition is often monotonous for many athletes, prompting more lethargy in practice than enthusiasm. In that regard, Anne Josephson recommends, "Mix up your lessons. Routines are useful, but doing the same thing each and every day is boring. Mix things up a bit from time to time._Work toward athletes' strengths. Focusing on improving weaknesses is a normal part of training. But *focusing on their strengths* can really boost an athlete's motivation."

Therefore, keep your players motivated by employing a variety of drills and sequences. In fact, involve the players themselves in the actual technique instruction by briefly discussing with them their opinions about the techniques you plan to cover. For example:
- "How would you block the defensive tackle from here?"
- "How would you get our opponents out of position on the serve?"
- "What am I doing wrong here, why can't I complete my stand up?"

This type of dialogue both eliminates confusion about the purpose or skill related to a specific technique and makes athletes feel more in control of their own practice responsibilities. Question-answer sessions can also help athletes improve their thinking skills and increase their motivation. Of course, when demonstrating techniques or strategies, the coach has several options, for example:
- The coach can demonstrate the technique.
- A highly-skilled player can demonstrate.
- Video can be used.
- Pictures and illustrations can be used.
- The coach can lecture and describe it.

Coaches should provide various demonstrations of important techniques (often from different angles) and possibly relate the new maneuver to some previously mastered skill. A continuous dialogue between coach and players should take place while skills are taught. As a result, the coach can discover who can add to the explanation and who may not understand it. This keeps players active and motivated during instruction, as opposed to being passive and sluggish observers.

Sport researcher Sara Robinson says, "[H]elping athletes feel good about what they are doing and feel competent in how they are performing is a key to increasing and sustaining motivation. When athletes don't feel they can perform well, or they are struggling physically, motivation can drop. *What can you do?* Give opportunities for your athletes to feel competent in their sport. For example, notice if an athlete is struggling with a skill—highlight what she is doing well and how she has already improved. You can also provide additional drills and training to help an athlete feel more prepared to execute the tougher skill."

Regardless of the drills you choose to do at practice, the key to keeping players engaged and motivated is to be sure to explain the *why*. In short, the athletes need to know why a technique must be performed a certain way or why the coaches are using selected training methods. "This means," says Dr. Alan Goldberg, "that you have to explain to them the necessity of their efforts. Simply telling an athlete to do something is nowhere near as effective as explaining to them how this exercise or drill will help them get closer to where they want to go."

"When [athletes] understand that what their learning now has a payoff to something they want to be able to do later, their motivation increases," says Anne Josephson. "[For example,] when your gymnasts are toiling away with a difficult conditioning assignment, remind them that those leg lifts will help them get their kip."

Greg Shelley of the Champion Coaches Network offers this perspective: "Keep your athletes informed as to when, where, how, and why (and WHY is most important)—people are not generally motivated to start (or finish) a task that is not clear in terms of when, where, how, or why. Take away any questions or doubts that your athletes may have by clearly and consistently communicating your expectations and intentions. Be clear as to when, where, and how . . . but most important, be sure your athletes know 'why' they are being asked to do something."

If athletes are clear about why the coaches are teaching and training a certain way, they feel more engaged at practice and more confident about their progress. Dr. Alan Goldberg summarizes this point: "Motivation is all about having a big enough 'why' or reason for doing something. If you have a big enough why, you can always find the 'how' to accomplish it . . . Remind them daily of this 'why.'"

Play Popular Music **47**

Playing popular music during practice has both advantages and disadvantages. The key advantage is that players will probably enjoy the music and lyrics and look forward to that interval of practice when the radio or music player is turned on. This can be done during scrimmaging, foul shooting, conducting drills, and running laps. And since the players' musical tastes change regularly, obligate them to bring in the music they'd like to hear (they'll probably bring in the player as well).

Andrew Hamilton states, "A particularly good way to motivate athletes in training and prior to competition is through the use of music they perceive to be inspirational." Sydney Olympics rowing Gold Medalist Tim Foster, now a respected coach, uses music to punctuate all of the indoor training sessions that he leads. Specifically, during circuit training or rowing ergometer intervals, he puts on loud/fast music, while during recovery periods he plays soft/slow music. Therefore, work and recovery times are regulated by music. Research from Brunel University indicates that this approach increases work output, reduces perceived exertion and improves in-task affect—the pleasure experienced during the activity."

The key disadvantage is the extra (and loud) noise, which either you or some players may not like. It's wise to have a manager stay near the music player and turn it off quickly on your command, when you need everyone's attention. You also should be cautious about allowing inappropriate lyrics to be played.

Music, especially the kind that is high-energy and up-beat, can serve to motivate most athletes, and if used judiciously, can be a welcome part of any practice.

Playing popular music during practice has both advantages and disadvantages.

Beloborod/Shutterstock.com

48 Manage the Time

As the coach for the Super Bowl champion Oakland Raiders, John Madden operated under two rules: (1) "Be on time" and (2) "Play like hell." The importance of time cannot be underrated by any coach. This doesn't refer just to the athletes' attendance or punctuality. Effective time management also depends on the coach planning the sequence of step-by-step activities that the team needs to cover. Once you arrange these steps, you need to consider the total time you have to accomplish them and then determine how much time the team can spend on each one. You should follow an organized practice schedule each day.

Being a motivational coach also requires the skill to "manipulate time," says a varsity coach with over 22 years of experience. "You have to have the ability to rapidly adjust practice and game plans that aren't working and paint a clear picture for the kids of what you want them to do."

You especially need to understand that time belongs to everyone, not just the coach. Sometimes, one coach's one-hour practice seems to go on for eternity while another's two-hour practice seems to end too quickly. "Practices are like classes," says former Norwalk (OH) High School athletic director Mike Grose. "In fact, practices may better prepare the students for their futures than do most classes. The competition and the practicing that take place help develop the student and lead them to success after they are out of school. That's why the coach has to be organized and knowledgeable at practice."

The length of practice should be determined based on several variables: the age of your athletes, their level of maturity, the stage of the season, their knowledge, and their physical condition. Generally, short practices are suitable for the younger (8-12) athlete, while longer ones are usually not a problem for the older, better conditioned players.

How much time you need for practice depends also on the kind of skills you need to teach. You should anticipate the questions and difficulties the kids will have prior to the practice and develop an interesting session that gets your athletes excited and eager to participate without delays. "An effective coach," says Larry Hoon, who had been a head wrestling coach for over 32 years, "runs an organized and efficient practice and simply has a plan for success. I'm also not afraid to venture beyond the teaching of moves or techniques and spend time getting to be friends with my kids."

You keep kids motivated if you start and end practice on time and follow a schedule that leads to positive outcomes. As long as your players see the time spent at practice is time spent efficiently and productively, they will participate with punctuality and enthusiasm. Effective time management is truly related to motivation.

Engage the Athletes' Mental Preparation

49

Coaches should devote as much practice time to developing their athletes' mental skills as they do the athletes' physical abilities. When athletes recognize they're being challenged to *think* as often as they're told to lift or run, their motivation increases. Much like we all enjoy brain teasers and riddles, coaches should engage their players' thinking skills as a way to motivate them. If you and your staff feel that changing any part of the practice routine will increase the probability that the players will be more mentally engaged to master necessary skills, then do it.

Indeed, it is okay to surprise them at times. Don't be afraid to change the warmup, the practice routine, or the format and intensity of each practice to prevent boredom or burnout. Quite a few athletes can be motivated by a spontaneous change in the practice format or content. This also prompts them to stay mentally focused.

The major objective of each practice is simply to take each player from their present skill level to a more advanced level. Their motivation to master advanced skills remains strong if these skills are not too complex or technical (they should be easy to understand and perform). Of course, the coaches should provide constant reinforcement or rewards after each attempt.

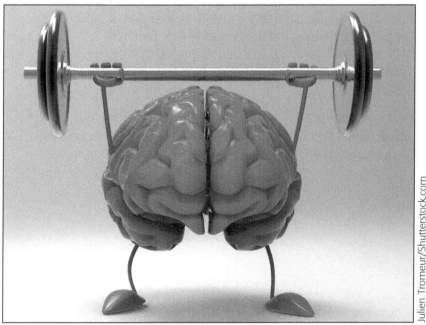

Julien Tromeur/Shutterstock.com

Coaches should devote as much practice time to developing their athletes' mental skills as they do the athletes' physical abilities.

Through the course of the practice, the coach should be cautious about fatigue. Indeed, as athletes' level of exhaustion increases, their mental engagement and level of motivation decrease. Heavy training sessions shouldn't be coupled with learning new skills. You should also avoid introducing new techniques late in the week or late in the season since this could prompt anxiety in some athletes who then could be too absorbed with their anxiety to learn what you're trying to teach.

Furthermore, practice should be a time for athletes to practice *mental skills* as well as physical ones. Their physical effort may require a lot of sweat; their mental effort requires constant concentration. Use the inquiry approach and ask them questions about a technique they tried in a previous competition ("Why did you do it that way?"); about each of the steps, let's say, in finishing a wrestling takedown; or about the offensive strategies the team should employ against the next opponent. In short, quiz them.

Sara Robinson states, "Motivation is defined as the direction and intensity of effort, which means that it's not just how much effort someone is putting in, but also what are they putting that effort toward? Your athletes may show up to practice, which suggests they're motivated, but if they lack focus and effort when they get there, then they may not be as motivated as you thought." Coaches should know how to keep their athletes mentally engaged at practice by providing "meaningful rationales and the nurturing of individuals' inner motivational resources."

Mental preparation should involve coaches circulating around the practice area and talking strategy with all athletes individually—freshmen, junior varsity, and varsity. This enables each athlete to receive a lot of feedback on their skills and, as a result, make greater improvements. When you talk to them as a group, ask for their input about strategies for defeating the next opponent or feedback about that day's practice. Prompt them to *think* in practice as often as possible. A college wrestler describes his wrestling coach as "hard working. He puts kids first. He teaches what it takes to win, how to *mentally* win."

Legendary hockey player Wayne Gretzky shows some great insight about the importance of mental preparation when he asserts, "A good hockey player plays where the puck is. A great hockey player plays where the puck is going to be."

Promote an Athletic Diet

50

Let's be honest: Rarely and unfortunately do we find teenagers (or adults!) who eat only nutritious and healthy foods. Fast food restaurants and junk food beckon to all of us daily, and it may seem impractical to suggest a healthy diet can motivate today's athlete. However, a coach who explains that a diet of complex carbohydrates, lean meats, fruits, and vegetables will lessen fatigue and injury during any competition can motivate athletes, once they experience the validity of this explanation. Athletes who eat junk food often have weak enzyme systems, and fatty foods typically take several days to break down. Athletes' motivation, therefore, can increase when they experience greater stamina and strength due to their diet.

Regardless of the sport, an ideal diet for most athletes involves avoiding saturated fats and processed foods. Moreover, if an athlete wants to increase muscle mass, they should consume higher levels of protein, while athletes who participate in more aerobic sports (for example, running and swimming) should take in more carbohydrates. Although most people enjoy foods and beverages that have high sugar and salt contents, athletes' physical conditioning and mental preparation improve when they consume the right foods.

According to most nutritionists, the right foods should include complex carbohydrates. In fact, fifty percent of an athlete's energy comes from carbohydrates. "Carbohydrate loading for three or four days before an event can help top up [their]

A coach can motivate athletes by promoting the connection between what and when athletes should eat and how this leads to success in competitions.

Elenadesign/Shutterstock.com

glycogen stores," says sports dietitian Joy Dubost, Ph.D. She recommends that athletes have a caloric intake in which 70% is from carbohydrates (e.g.., breads, cereals, pasta, fruit) and that they avoid eating anything three to four hours before competing to give their stomachs time to empty.

A coach can motivate athletes by promoting the connection between what and when athletes should eat and how this leads to success in competitions. If athletes can recognize that they can resist fatigue and outmuscle opponents due to their diet, they should feel motivated.

To battle fatigue, athletes should avoid milk, saturated fat, trans fat, sugars, and excessive amounts of protein in their diet because they are difficult to break down and force the body to use its energy to digest them. Athletes, of course, will need that energy for competitions.

To be sure, the best diet for athletes will vary, depending on the physical demands of their sport, but, regardless of the athletic activity, they need to consume enough calories to make up for the amount they burn off during practice and games. Coaches would be wise to have a sports or school dietitian address the team to provide the right information specifically tailored to their sport.

Most coaches should realize their athletes will eat junk food and fast food, but coaches should urge their players to do this only in moderation. Coaches should also inform parents of the need for a balanced diet and recommend, in fact, the best food choices for that sport. For instance, since most football players seek to gain strength and muscle mass, those coaches might suggest foods that contain high levels of protein, like fish (especially tuna and salmon), lean beef, beans, broccoli, spinach, yogurt, and almonds.

Former champion professional golfer Jack Nicklaus recalls, "Perhaps no one realizes how important a good diet has been for me. I can't describe how important it is . . . [When] you change your diet, you start feeling good, and you don't even mind looking in the mirror. Gradually, you rise to a different physical and mental level." Ultimately, coaches should do additional research about the link between nutrition and sports performance, convey this information to their athletes, and emphasize as well the importance of water for proper hydration.

In addition, coaches should plan pre-game and post-game meals carefully to motivate their players. You might suggest that your athletes read the book *Eat to Win: The Sports Nutrition Bible* by Dr. Robert Haas. This book offers cogent advice to athletes on a nutrition program that can increase their energy and endurance, with additional information on improving fitness and preventing injuries.

Demonstrate Your Knowledge

51

The coach has to project credibility (i.e., that the coach knows the skills and techniques and variables. The coach is *experienced.*) and believability. The key is that kids are convinced the techniques and strategies you teach can work for them. The coach also has to stay in control. In other words, he is prepared for potential interruptions, annoying distractions, and unexpected questions, especially when teaching very technical skills. A coach like this motivates athletes to compete with confidence.

The athletes must respect your status as their coach, so establish your credibility as quickly as possible. Credibility is probably most important at the beginning of the season to get athletes motivated and excited. Raphael Taylor participated on the varsity football, wrestling, and track teams at Cleveland Heights (OH) High School and always checked to see if his coach "knows what's best, knows what he's doing, and knows how to go about it. I made it to States because my coach got to know me better than I know myself. He knew what I was capable of."

Coaches can demonstrate their credibility in several ways, including the following:
- Show an effective knowledge of strategies.
- Be dynamic and enthusiastic.
- Remain confident in every situation.
- Treat all athletes in a fair and consistent manner.
- Have a history of positive team performances and/or personal success.

FrankHH/Shutterstock.com

The coach has to project credibility (i.e., that the coach knows the skills and techniques and variables. The coach is experienced.*) and believability.*

Athletes must see you as someone competent enough to lead them and even willing to take risks to improve their individual performances. One veteran coach adopted a wrestling program at a high school that had rarely experienced any kind of success. His credibility came from "building a successful program at the school. I saw that I had to create an environment with a family approach. A coach has to be a leader. Demanding. Enthusiastic. A motivator. A coach in today's society must work *with* players, not be their dictator."

When you increase your athletes' knowledge base and when they know about their sport's specific most updated techniques and strategies, the more motivated they'll feel about competing. A varsity track athlete claims, "I'm motivated by a coach who has knowledge of the sport and is able to communicate this to us in an intense way that is still fun and interesting." At practice, players should look upon their coach as the expert who knows what they need to do in order to win. This, therefore, involves detailed preparation for each day.

In conclusion, coaches should be students of their sport themselves. Updated textbooks, coaching clinics, top-notch videos, and effective dialoging with other coaches can improve coaches' understanding of their sport. According to Richard Greene, a former Illinois principal, the coach has to keep learning. "The coach must first possess a thorough knowledge of the sport and be able to communicate that knowledge well. If I have to fire a coach it's usually because they are abusive, poorly organized, or poorly prepared in the knowledge of the game." A varsity athlete at University (HI) High School sums it up well: "An effective coach is someone who knows the game and the competition like the back of his hand. He has to be able to devote his time to coaching and making the team better both in-season and off-season. He has to push athletes to strive to be better and never give up."

Use First Names 52

At every practice, every player should be acknowledged in some personal way by at least one coach, and during that dialogue, the coach should use the athlete's first name.

Why? Coaching is as much about how you establish relationships and rapport with your athletes as it is the skills you teach them. Probably more. Using first names prompts a more personal and attached relationship between you and the athlete, and most often, when they hear their first names used, athletes are more attentive, on task, and motivated!

Since practice involves a continuous communication between coaches and athletes, enhance that communication (and motivation) by using first names as often as possible, much like a classroom teacher does. This can be done when greeting athletes, teaching them, and even in matters of discipline. Furthermore, doing so can prompt players to see you as someone who cares. Anne Josephson asserts, "As social beings, we are all thrive on connection. The more connected, the more motivated we are to do well."

You should also learn the names of your athletes' parents, their brothers and sisters, maybe even how they all spent their summer vacations. When you take an active interest in each player's family, that family takes an active interest in your program. Talk to your athletes and their parents after matches, during the "down" times at tournaments, or at other sporting events. As you use those brief opportunities to befriend them, allow them to get to know you. As you develop these relationships, you build motivation.

Suzanne Tucker/Shutterstock.com

Coaching is as much about how you establish relationships and rapport with your athletes as it is the skills you teach them.

Designate a Winning Time

Developing different ways to motivate a team is certainly an ongoing challenge. Each season may require new methods, but the experienced coach realizes this. A new season often means you have a new team (seniors have graduated, newcomers have joined) and a fresh group to teach how to be successful. Consider, therefore, allowing them to *teach themselves*.

Dominique Stasulli sees the value of what I call *"winning time"* approach. "Coaches can also boost autonomy in their athletes by encouraging self-monitoring, performance reflection, and honest evaluation of physical and emotional well-being." The "winning time" strategy enables athletes to share ownership of their physical and mental preparation with the coaches and to select their own methods for self-improvement. This strategy can enhance their personal motivation.

How does "winning time" work? Allow athletes a 10-15 minute time span either at the middle or near the end of each practice for them to work on mastering their weakest skills, a period in which they can work together or alone on the techniques or skills that they need to master in order to make themselves better competitors. Giving them free time to use as they see best to make themselves better athletes is a unique motivator, one few coaches may feel comfortable employing. In short, the athletes are designing the foundation for their own success.

The "winning time" strategy enables athletes to share ownership of their physical and mental preparation with the coaches and to select their own methods for self-improvement.

You could introduce "winning time" with the same statements Dr. Jim Taylor uses when he speaks to athletes: "Your choice [of an activity] will dictate the amount of time and effort you will put into your sport and how good an athlete you will ultimately become." In a reference to gymnasts, for example, Anne Josephson recommends, "Let athletes choose between two different conditioning exercises that target the same muscle group or decide in which order they want to work their skills. Small tweaks that give the athlete some autonomy may lead to huge gains in motivation."

Typically, you'll notice groups of three or four choosing an activity (e.g., running laps or hitting the blocking sled), and then motivating each other until it's completed. It is not uncommon to observe seniors teaching freshmen or the talented kids encouraging the untalented ones.

The only rule is that all athletes must stay active (running, drilling, jumping rope, lifting, etc.) during this session. This time is allotted for them to work on skills, not rest. The coaches can also give individual attention to some athletes during this short period. When athletes are self-directed like this (while under your observation), you can provide more individualized instruction and correct their mistakes. This situation can also enable them to take some element of control over their own skill development and improvement as an athlete.

Clearly, what happens to athletes at practice has a major influence on what happens for them in competitions. Coaches must make their players recognize the importance of practicing with intensity and diligence, especially when they can choose the activity. Players have to be directed to take responsibility for their own success in practice, and when you let them do so, you increase their motivation.

54 Allow a Day Off

Don't be afraid to give a day off. Coaches have to be flexible. On some days, you may discover that your team is troubled or concerned about some school or social issue. It's interfering with their concentration on the tasks you've planned for practice, and they're sluggish through every opening drill. Be ready, therefore, to talk about it and make adjustments. If team members still appear troubled or upset, release this psychological burden by sharing it with them. Counter any negative feelings by giving them reasons to be excited about the upcoming competition and reviewing team (and possibly individual goals. More importantly, don't add to their anxiety; instead, have an open forum discussion about it or release them from practice altogether. They will probably return the next day more motivated for practice and more convinced you are a coach who truly cares about their welfare.

Don't be afraid to give a day off.

xtock/Shutterstock.com

Keep an Even Keel

55

Often, an athletic season can be described as peaks and valleys: typically, achievements and disappointments. Coaches could, for instance, struggle with the disappointment associated with failing to win games, to satisfy the needs of administrators, and to accomplish goals. Maybe they will have to confront poor behavior exhibited by some of players or worse, the loss of a key player due to injury. All these events can lessen *a coach's* motivation and indirectly the motivation of the athletes.

That said, coaches must keep an even keel to avoid the emotional rollercoaster of the season. This will require stamina and determination, plus understanding that conflicts are inevitable whenever large groups of people come together, even if they all are dedicated to the same general goal, and that few teams go undefeated forever.

Furthermore, rarely will all persons in your program have identical expectations, interests, or timetables. Every coach, therefore, should be prepared to confront criticism, so that it does not affect their athletes' motivation. Any form of disapproval can cause even the most confident coach to feel inadequate, uncertain, or unmotivated. "Motivation is a tricky subject," says Anne Josephson. "On one hand, it is a feeling. And no one can make another person feel a certain way. It is up to individuals to find their motivation. However, motivation is also skill, one that can be developed or depressed by the teachers, coaches, and parents in an athlete's life."

Coaches must keep an even keel to avoid the emotional rollercoaster of the season.

Coaching is a way to contribute to young people's lives. Few adults in their lives help them set goals, train them to achieve those objectives, and then reward them for their efforts. Sports offer athletes a wonderful opportunity for physical, mental, and social growth. You are the catalyst for this growth.

You are probably their key motivator. This is why you need a system in place that enables you to deal effectively with the low points in a season where problems are solved in a positive way and losses are handled so that all athletes stay motivated and on target to achieving their goals. Dr. Alan Goldberg says, "Motivation is a key element of getting positive results in the sports arena. And I'm not just talking about winning! It's the quality that will propel athletes to keep giving it their all, as long as there's time on the clock, to bounce back after failures or setbacks, and to do everything they possibly can to perform to their full potential."

First, take responsibility for solving any problem or dealing with any loss, without rationalizing or placing any blame on someone else. Second, remain patient, objective, and understanding, even if the problem is on-going or the loss is especially upsetting. Third, possibly with the help of your coaching staff, come up with multiple solutions and strategies for dealing with the problem or loss. Finally, make a public commitment to solving the conflict or overcoming the loss. This leads to a more diligent endeavor on your part in handling it and, in turn, models the approach you want your athletes to take when they confront adversity.

Never lose control of yourself in front of your athletes or allow emotion, especially excitement or anger, to cloud your actions. Remain calm and objective, even if the problem is personal or the loss happened in the championship game. Events like this are simply part of the profession. Successful coaches never remain discouraged or indulge in self-pity.

In conclusion, reducing the emotions we attach to losing and minimizing their disruptive influence are crucial to effective motivation. Understand that you don't have to win championships right away, and the athletes most often will forgive you for your errors, if you forgive them for theirs. As a former coach in the NFL, Sam Rutigliano has seen all the highs and lows of coaching. Rutigliano sees the way to a rewarding career through finding "a middle level." He warns that "a lot of good men become Jekyll and Hydes, and everyone they touch suffers." Thus, keep an even keel. Don't get too excited about winning or too disappointed with a loss. Your athletes need to see a coach who maintains their composure and poise, regardless of the outcome of the competition.

Arrange Pep Assemblies

56

Pep assemblies seem to be part of the environment of nearly every school in the country. Some are brief, simple affairs where players are introduced and the head coach makes a speech, while others are extravagant events involving confetti, cheers, fireworks, music, and speakers like local politicians, administrators, coaches, and team captains. Regardless of the format, well-structured pep assemblies, whether they are in the high school gym or in the football stadium, are important to the motivation of athletes.

I suggest making a pep assembly as dramatic as possible. Certainly one part of it is to introduce players so consider unique ways to do this. For example, have basketball players in uniform emerge from the locker room through a tunnel of cheerleaders and the pep band and break through a paper hoop. Arrange for the golf team to enter the rally, as long as it is outside, on golf carts. Cross country and track athletes (in uniform) can run in.

The point? Avoid the traditional "line up and step forward when I call your name" introduction. Instead, get creative in how players are introduced.

Well-structured pep assemblies, whether they are in the high school gym or in the football stadium, are important to the motivation of athletes.

debra hughes/Shutterstock.com

Music is very important. Play the students' favorite music during the rally from a speaker system or have the school pep band perform in between introductions. Don't worry about students dancing in the bleachers—that means they're involved and engaged in the rally. In fact, you do not want the other students just sitting passively. You want them yelling, cheering, and stomping.

To accomplish this at my former school, we used a lot of audience participation. Students from each grade were pulled from the stands to engage in various contests. For example, who can throw a football the farthest? Who can sink the most free throws? Who can win a game of musical chairs? Use wacky relays on tricycles, pie eating contests, and dance contests. You can even make this a "Battle of the Classes."

An effective way to boost the student body's interest and educate them about your sport is to have an all-school assembly, where you introduce all squad members and display athletes in action. You can use a video on a large screen, a slide show, or some players who demonstrate an actual contest (for example, two wrestlers wrestling each other), which you choreograph beforehand.

I also know of some pep assemblies that have involved skits, bonfires, and even motorcycles. The intent is not to divert attention from the athletes but to heighten the excitement in the student body about the team and the season.

Potential guest speakers could include school administrator(s), the mayor (or another popular politician), a professional athlete, a celebrity, the booster club president, and the varsity captains. All should have one focus: praise the players and wish them good luck.

Don't neglect cheerleaders, the pep club, the dance team, and the marching band. You can even involve the drama club or theater department to perform skits or scenes. Just be sure all these groups are given enough advance notice and their dance or skit is brief. Again, keep the focus on the athletes.

A typical and successful rally should last 30-40 minutes and be fast-paced. Students and staff in the school and community members should know about it at least 3-4 weeks in advance through posters, flyers, and p.a. announcements. Finally, ask your athletes what they would like to have happen at the pep rally—give them some ownership, especially for their introduction. They might have some great ideas.

And at the end of the rally, they should definitely feel motivated!

Travel in Style

57

Most coaches and athletes are used to the long yellow school bus or the cramped, dingy van. The bench seats can be uncomfortable on long trips and the exhaust smell sickening. Why not, instead, travel in style and surprise (and motivate) your team by traveling to a major competition in limousines or a chartered bus?

Certainly, a cost is involved. However, employing a special fundraiser or asking the booster club or a local organization to pay for this are ways to handle that cost. Once community members recognize the importance of the competition, they may be encouraged to donate to the athletic department to enable the team to travel in style.

Your players will appreciate the special attention given to them and, in turn, be motivated to perform in style as well.

Why not travel in style and surprise (and motivate) your team by traveling to a major competition in limousines or a chartered bus?

58 Organize Home Competitions in an Impressive Manner

One varsity athlete claims, "I'm motivated by performing well in front of a big crowd. I like being a part of the competition." Her statement emphasizes the importance of conducting home competitions in an impressive manner. You can accomplish this by employing the talents of various individuals and groups.

The first key person to involve is the athletic director. You will need their approval before making any arrangements. Confirm what is acceptable and what isn't, and do this in writing, so no confusion exists concerning your plans for conducting the home competition in such way that the athletes get even more motivated about competing.

The next person to consult is the audiovisual director at the school. This person can arrange music, special lighting, and staging for the competition. You may want a spotlight to highlight players when they are introduced or play certain songs during any breaks.

Ask the announcer to read a motivational script during the introduction or a list of announcements during time outs in the game to highlight certain players or events.

Arrange for the art department to paint signs, banners, or posters to be placed in the gym or on the fence outside on the football field. Be sure, though, that these are appropriate and don't violate any guidelines related to sportsmanship.

Assistant coaches can lead specific groups of athletes onto the field or into the gym to acknowledge those players personally and allow fans to cheer for them.

Also utilize cheerleaders, the marching or pep band, the pep or school spirit club, and possibly the student council to increase school spirit and attendance at the game. Ask the advisors to participate and let them determine the way they'd like to contribute. All these groups, working in unison, can make for an impressive showing for the fans and your players.

Keep in mind, however, Dr. Alan Goldberg's advice: "90% of motivation happens in practice from day #1. 5-10% of motivation gets done just before the big game/ race/match. Unless you are working every day at being a motivator, the gimmicks and talks that you pull out on game day will be ineffective."

And finally, at home competitions, it is especially important to make sure everyone, if possible, has a chance to compete. Few athletes are motivated by sitting on the bench.

Prepare for Failure **59**

Coaches have to teach athletes that failure is a word; winning is an attitude.

Everyone makes mistakes, but the better competitors don't make excuses. The very best athletes take responsibility for their losses, correct their mistakes, and move on. They don't blame others, nor do they dwell on the loss. More importantly, these athletes return to practice with an immediate incentive to improve their weak points. "It may sound strange," says Bob Richards, an Olympic gold medalist in the pole vault, "but many champions are made champions by setbacks. They are champions because they've been hurt. Their experience moved them and pulled out this fighting spirit, making them what they are."

The following is another applicable quote: "The child's philosophy is a true one. He does not despise the bubble because it burst; he immediately sets to work to blow another one."

The fear of failure can affect athletes in diverse ways. You might have, in fact, athletes on your team who continually claim injuries—real or imagined, minor or major—in order to avoid competition and potential failure. To these types of athletes, the competition is more threatening than the hurt they may have. Some may try to become injured, since only an injury can provide them some of the psychological nurturing that they cannot receive elsewhere. In this way, the athlete gets sympathy, relief from the competition, attention for the injury, and possibly a heroic stature in the eyes of their peers. This is the kid who exaggerates a limp or grimaces at the slightest touch. All of these actions are often intended to cover up a lack of confidence (and motivation). In addition, they could be trying to punish themselves for failing to reach a goal or live up to expectations. They are simply afraid to fail.

Anne Josephson recommends that coaches "normalize failure." If you do this, you can help eliminate your players' fear of failure which can affect their motivation. Dr. Goldberg agrees. "Teach your athletes that failures and setbacks are a necessary part of the learning process and not a cause for embarrassment or quitting," he says. "Model this attitude, and you'll motivate your athletes to take risks and really go for it. If you jump in an athlete's face whenever he messes up, you'll demotivate him and get him worrying about failing."

The coach needs to understand both this athlete's fear of losing and their feelings of inferiority. Effective strategies would be to keep the injured athlete at practice to train healthy body parts, work at weak points, and build confidence (e.g., "You're showing some real strength there, just keep doing your best").

Also, do not reprimand any athlete for faking an injury. If this is the case, the athlete is sending an obvious signal that there is a more serious problem below the surface, often a personal one that may have nothing to do with you, the team, or the sport. Communication and understanding are the keys in this instance, to straightening out this type of problem and redirecting the athlete's motivation toward having a successful season. Dominique Stasulli, writing for SimpliFaster, notes that some coaches unfortunately have "an ego-driven belief that enduring pain and winning are the strongest measures of an athlete's reputation and success."

Athletes develop at different levels and times through their careers, and failure is typically part of the growth process. The key in this instance, is to provide all athletes with meaningful and rewarding experiences, to help them see that losing a competition only proves what didn't work that time. According to the Association for Sport Psychology in the article "Motivating Young Athletes," "The best way to motivate [athletes] is to make them feel skilled and valued. This is especially important for young athletes who are just learning the skills and strategies of a sport." Athletes have to realize that losing only adds weight to their lives if they let it. They can still be winners, no matter what the scoreboard indicates after the game.

Therefore, have a pre-planned response for potential failures and consider writer Lyman Fertig's advice: "If I could have one hope for our young people as they go out into the world, it would be this: I hope they fail. I hope they fail at something that is important to them, for failure, like nothing else, is able to stimulate the right kind of person to that extra action that always makes all the difference." Fertig truly understands what we need to instill in our athletes: winning is found not on a scoreboard but in a person's character.

Prepare for Excuses

It's unfortunate, but we may see too many of our athletes make excuses for their losses. They may rationalize the defeat. Even worse, they may blame others. Do not let them! This is anti-motivation and can debilitate any athlete or team if allowed to continue.

Excuse-making should be anticipated and never ignored. When it occurs, do not dismiss the excuse or try to make the athlete feel wrong. Instead, find out why the player feels that way and seek a positive outcome. Get the complaint or issue out in the open and deal with it in a mature way, possibly in an open team discussion. The criticism that the athlete(s) has may be fair and justified, but the player must also be part of the resolution. The late Alabama football coach Paul Bear Bryant understood this and recommended, "When you make a mistake, there are only three things you should ever do about it: (1) admit it; (2) learn from it; and (3) don't repeat it."

Tell your athletes this quote from acclaimed poet Nikki Giovanni: "Mistakes are a fact of life. It is the response to the error that counts."

Excuse-making should be anticipated and never ignored.

Ivelin Radkov/Shutterstock.com

61 **Avoid Making Comparisons**

When I entered high school and joined the freshman football team, the coaches immediately began comparing me to my older brother who had been a star linebacker. I think they were somewhat surprised I lacked his talent and ability, and when I missed a tackle, they'd chide me for not performing the way my brother had. I finished the season but never played football again.

Unless it is done in a consistently positive way, comparing athletes in any way can lessen an athlete's motivation. Writing for the National Alliance for Youth Sports, Sara Robinson notes, "Each athlete is motivated differently. Some athletes will be motivated by internal factors, such as the love of playing or improving their skills, while others are motivated by external factors, for example, getting praise, winning a trophy." Coaches need to recognize these differences in their athletes and avoid making comparisons between them.

Dr. Alan Goldberg has a similar viewpoint: "Comparisons almost always make athletes feel badly about themselves, which kills their motivation and engenders intrasquad rivalry & unhealthy competition." If you treat each athlete as an individual, they will feel more comfortable with their position on the team and more motivated to prove themselves in competition.

Making comparisons between one team and another, one player and another, or one season and another can most often dampen a current player's motivation. According to Dominique Stasulli, "Coaches can develop psychologically motivated athletes with positive self-regard by creating self-worth and a sense of belonging and by limiting judgmental comparisons to other athletes' success."

Unless it is done in a consistently positive way, comparing athletes in any way can lessen an athlete's motivation.

Repair Breakdowns

What about those athletes who never seem to fulfill their potential or, even worse, want to quit? You may hear from them, "I can't win. He's [the opponent] too good." This type of athlete is often an erratic performer who may look like a champion one day and a chump the next. For them, the underlying problem often is an intense fear of not measuring up or of not performing successfully in the next competition. It may be that they dread being successful, although they are aware that their teammates and coaches are ready to congratulate them for any achievement. Their motivation is broken and needs repair.

In this instance, a variety of factors can be involved, some of which you may not be able to control. However, you can deal effectively with the athlete who is troubled by the mental or physical strains of the sport and may want to quit. Often, quitting occurs when the athlete is struggling with recent failures. A knowledgeable and caring coach should recall a positive moment for this athlete and review it with them. Don't lie to them or give false praise but certainly point out improvement.

Regarding the physical demands of the sport that may be overwhelming the athlete, the coach needs to explain that the athlete isn't alone. All athletes, even the great ones, hate the physical punishment required in preparing to compete. Mark Lieberman, a former NCAA national champion wrestler, says, "You have to be willing to pay the price . . . It's hard work and hardly any fun, but it can also be intensely satisfying."

Regarding the physical demands of the sport that may be overwhelming the athlete, the coach needs to explain that the athlete isn't alone.

Comeback Images/Shutterstock.com

On occasion, athletes want to quit because the satisfaction and reward of wearing the uniform is overshadowed by the realization that they are obligated to work harder than they ever have before in order to put on that uniform. These kinds of athletes need to understand that hard work produces success, but not necessarily wins.

Other typical breakdowns can be the result of having poor relations with teammates and communication problems with the coach, among others. There are, in truth, many more reasons why athletes suffer breakdowns or want to quit than can be expressed in a single segment of this book. In reality, a number of relatively prominent ones exist. Furthermore, quitting often is not an individual decision made by the athlete. Others—family, friends, teachers—may have influenced it, but overall, athletes choose to quit when:

- Their peers tell them to.
- They resent their teammates.
- They resent or distrust the coach.
- Alcohol or drugs have become more important.
- The sport is no longer enjoyable to them (burn out).
- Family problems interfere.
- They fear injury or the physical grind.
- Academic problems surface.

When pressed up against themselves, many athletes decide to quit to relieve the burden of confronting their own inadequacies.

In that instance, what should the coach do? Initially, you should try to talk out the problem. Sometimes, the athlete has set such a difficult goal that the challenge to accomplish it has overwhelmed them. You can help set a more realistic goal and encourage persistence to reach it. The root cause will always relate to one or several of his intrinsic motivational needs that are not being satisfied. Anne Josephson, writing in *In Coaching, Psychology*, recommends that coaches reference the growth-mindset approach and "compliment athletes over things that they can control (like attendance, effort, and attitude), so they understand that they can persist at a challenge in order to improve."

If it is failure that is interfering, model how to cope with failure and emphasize skill improvement, rather than winning. Clarify and highlight those moments when the athlete has been successful and allow them to "savor" those achievements. And definitely involve the parents. Invite them and any other athletes to talk to the athlete. Above all, keep a positive, patient attitude. A junior varsity football player is even more succinct: "A motivational coach won't let you quit, even if you aren't good at the sport."

Motivate the Uncoachable Athlete **63**

Coaches need to recognize that some athletes shuffle passively towards competitions, while others strut with overconfidence. As a rule, it can be a struggle to motivate athletes who lack commitment to you, the program, or their teammates. However, if you identify and promote their intrinsic needs, they can be productive members of your program and achieve their individual potential.

Whatever your coaching level, you may discover at least one athlete who wants to be on the team but doesn't want to be coached. In a report from researcher Andrew Hamilton, "a study examining the relationship between athletes' goal orientations and their levels of intrinsic and extrinsic motivation indicated that British collegiate athletes with task-related or personal mastery goals were far more likely to report high self-determination than athletes with ego-orientated or social comparison-type goals." The latter type of athlete is self-centered and socially flawed and could be, in short, deemed "uncoachable."

Frequently, coaches define "coachability" in terms of how well the athlete follows directions or acquires the skills they teach. Coaches may expect coachable athletes to have a good rapport with them, to respect the coaching staff's decisions, and to request help from the coaches if they have personal problems. The uncoachable athlete may want no input from the coaches.

When problems occur, coaches who are not flexible sometimes doubt the athlete's willingness to be coached. In this case, there are several key signs of athletes being uncoachable, including the following:
- Do they refuse to train with the rest of the team?
- Do they sulk, whine, or complain when things don't go their way?
- Do they behave in a belligerent way or get in fights with teammates?
- Do they often fail to try their best at practice or in competitions?
- Do they "showboat" during competitions or berate opponents?
- Do they refuse to adhere to any training schedule or fail to be punctual at meetings or practice?
- Does that athlete demonstrate disrespect for you or constantly test your authority?

This type of athlete may continually avoid you or make excessive demands (e.g., for special equipment or extra time). The uncoachable athlete may find fault with the way you manage the team and disrupts practice to argue aspects of technique or strategy. Instructions may have to be repeated, equipment or uniforms have to replaced, and confrontations with teammates have to be arbitrated. Suddenly, it is not one athlete's motivation that you must deal with but every team member's.

Such disruptive behaviors make everyone uncomfortable and tense. Dr. Bruce C. Ogilvie, Ph.D., and Dr. Thomas A. Tutko, Ph.D., researched athletes like this and published their results in *Problem Athletes and How to Handle Them*. They concluded that coachability is one of the most essential characteristics for superior athletic performances.

When confronted with such an athlete, a common first reaction is simple: dismiss them from the team. But if you see the potential for change, then there is a viable approach for dealing with this type of individual. The key point is to determine the athlete's level of trust. Maybe, they have been exploited before and now find it difficult to have any kind of an effective rapport with a coach.

Ironically, when the flexible coach approaches the uncoachable athlete in a sincere attempt to communicate, the dialogue may backfire. For the coach, the conversation involves advice and compassion. To the athlete, it's criticism. What, then, should you do? Ogilivie and Tutko offer the following guidelines:

- Be reliable by saying what you will do and doing what you say.
- React positively when the athlete offers reasonable suggestions for change.
- Be judicious when scheduling practices.
- Give athletes options.

Krakenimages.com/Shutterstock.com

Coaches need to recognize that some athletes shuffle passively towards competitions, while others strut with overconfidence.

- Don't make promises you can't keep.
- Avoid being judgmental; show tolerance for their inadequacies.
- Don't overemphasize their failures, especially as a means to change their inappropriate behavior. Be cautious when using criticism.
- Don't get into power struggles (or be manipulated).
- Remind the athlete of your position as coach; your obligation above anything else is to the team as a whole.
- Negate any hostility with a calm and disarming demeanor.
- Don't give the uncoachable athlete responsibility as a means of changing their behavior (like making them a team captain).
- Don't lose patience.
- Don't let their actions negate your ability to coach the rest of the team.
- Don't be afraid to dismiss the athlete from the team, regardless of their talent or potential.

It takes time, effort, and flexibility on the coach's part to deal with a difficult athlete, and it may or may not turn out that it is time well spent. A veteran coach who has had winning teams at three different schools is always willing to work with these kinds of athletes. "A coach has to remember," he says, "how high school really was. A coach must always be ready to communicate and be flexible. Patience is also important. Sometimes, you have to sacrifice personal time or adjust your priorities on what is really important."

In their research, Ogilvie and Tutko discovered that these types of athletes often operate under a feeling of fear. The wise coach, therefore, should "develop a subtle technique for talking about fear and its effects upon performance . . . Coaches who expose their own personal fears as experiences in athletics pave the most sensitive roads to dealing with this emotion." This fear often surfaces in athletes who are experiencing some type of pressure or stress.

Potential conflicts with an athlete are lessened when you get clear about specific goals (What do they exactly want to accomplish?), either through conversation or questionnaire sheet administered at the first team meeting. Next, in order to change behavior, discover why they're behaving that way. Show sympathy and tolerance but not resignation. Then, present options that are both non-threatening and different (they can't be the same ones they have heard from parents or other coaches). Decide together and follow through, until the athlete realizes they can gain more from ending the conflict than from continuing it. The ultimate goal should be to motivate this athlete, not dismiss them.

64 Require Physical Preparation

Young athletes have to be told that getting in shape means experiencing various levels of discomfort. No one likes to work to exhaustion, yet being an athlete often requires daily doses of fatigue. Former NFL running back Mike Pruitt says, "In order to succeed greatly, you have to sacrifice greatly. Nobody ever said it would be easy."

You probably have discovered that working athletes too hard in practice discourages some of them, but working them too lightly leaves them physically unprepared for competitions. Your players can find practice to be an enjoyable, motivational, and enriching experience, regardless of its difficulty, if you do one or more of the following:

- Occasionally, let team leaders run practice.
- Can list examples of matches where their physical conditioning has resulted in victory.
- Can point out how tapping into physical reservoirs of energy produces power.
- Have them pretend that "Today is the last practice of the season. Make it your best!"
- Use a variety of challenging drills.
- Know when to push and when to call it a day.

Take, for example, Carl Lewis, probably one of the best Olympic track athletes of all time. When an interviewer asked Tom Tellez, his coach, to summarize the factors that prompted Lewis' phenomenal success, he said, "I work on mechanics. You prepare the athlete mentally by preparing him physically."

A high school football player says, "I love competition, and I want to stay in shape. That's what motivates me. During the summer, I set a goal to get in 200 hours of work. I got in 241 hours. My coach helped a lot. He always has a positive attitude—he's very optimistic, very motivational."

Since preparing for any competition is seldom fun for athletes, and because it normally involves extensive physical and mental effort, acknowledge that fact and be ready to recognize those athletes who maintain a positive outlook through the grind of practice. Point out and praise those times when they are successful at practice to build their confidence and increase their motivation. Thomas Edison's famous quote applies in this instance: "Genius is one percent inspiration and 99 percent perspiration . . . [none] of my inventions came by accident; they came by work."

To be sure, this advice is going to take persistence because too often the local newspapers, radio, and television stations are more interested in professional teams, but send them media releases anyway and invite them to do brief profiles on the team as a whole or some outstanding or unique athletes. Almost all college, high school, and middle school players are motivated when they see this coverage.

Provide this information to the media in a news-style format and encourage them to attend the next match or tournament. Keep sending these media releases (see Figure 65-1), whether the information is published or not. Contact these news sources by telephone and try especially to make a friend with them. If you can get one reporter or broadcaster on your side, their coverage can do wonders for your program.

Work to get the athletes' names and accomplishments in the newspaper or on the radio and inform them (and their parents) when it happens. Invite the media to interview you and/or your better players. Subsequently, send a thank you note to the media for their coverage. You should also invite media personnel to your awards program at the end of the season and write a thank you letter for the publicity they provided during the season (see Figure 65-2).

DONOT6_STUDIO/Shutterstock.com

Work to get the athletes' names and accomplishments in the newspaper or on the radio and inform them (and their parents) when it happens.

High School Media Release

To _____ Date_____

From Head Coach _____

Re: _____ Invitational Wrestling Tournament Placers

The _____ _____ High School Spartans won the team championship trophy at their own invitational tournament ahead of a field of 16 teams on Saturday, _____(date).

The following athletes achieved placement:

Brian Smith (106)   Champion

Bill Miller (119)   Runner up

Matt Musarra (125)   Runner up

Mike Connely (135)   Fourth Place

Herb Adkins (140)   Champion

Pat Campolieti (145)   Champion

Joe Daugherty (152)   Third Place

Greg Leinweber (171)   Champion

Dan Agresta (HWT)   Fourth Place

The Spartan's current dual meet record is 5-1, and the squad competes next in a quad match at Norwalk High School on _____ (date)

For further information call _____ anytime between _____ and _____.

Figure 65.1 An example of a media release

Dear _____

Your coverage of our game against _____ High School
effectively described the competitive effort put forth by both teams. It was an exciting
match, and all the athletes, coaches, and parents associated with our program are grateful
you reported on it.

We are especially pleased that you highlighted several individual performances. Overall,
your article was informative and entertaining. Our parents, students, and staff look forward
to reading more like it.

Again, thanks for the recent article and your continued coverage of the
_____ High School boy's basketball team.

With appreciation,

Figure 65-2. An example of a thank you letter to the media

66 Use the School's Public Address

Each week during the season, you should use your school's public address system to highlight and acknowledge the accomplishments of your team and individual players. In doing so, you bring the athletes both recognition in front of their peers and a sense of pride for their participation on the team. Hearing their names and then receiving compliments from classmates are very motivational to young athletes. Be sure you do this on a regular basis and vary the names of your players as much as possible. Also, use clear, typed, and uncomplicated language so the P.A. announcers, who usually are students, can easily read the announcement. See Figure 66-1 as an example.

A special congratulations to the varsity girls tennis team! Number one singles Jenny Jones won her tenth match of the season, and the doubles team of Margaret Mitchell and Christine Smith defeated their opponents 6-0, 6-1. The Mitchell-Smith combination is undefeated for the season. Also winning their matches were Sarah Brett and Emily Lee. The varsity girls' tennis team is next in action on Thursday at 4:00 PM in DeSan Park. You should check out the best team in the league.

Figure 66-1. An example of a P.A. announcement

cigdem/Shutterstock.com

Each week during the season, you should use your school's public address system to highlight and acknowledge the accomplishments of your team and individual players.

Give Pep Talks

67

When many coaches consider a pre-game locker room pep talk, they get a vision of Knute Rockne's "win this one for the Gipper" speech. Not only does such drama not motivate all athletes, many times, it isn't even needed. In fact, such a speech might even be counterproductive.

Pep talks need not be emotional tirades. More often, they should be business-like in tone and format, where the coach expresses, as clearly and as briefly as possible, what awaits the athletes and what is expected of them. Whether the coach wants to provoke their athletes or not, the comments should be straightforward and honest. The coach must demonstrate calmness and confidence, especially when the athletes seem tense or uncertain, and use emotion only if the timing seems right.

Coaches should adhere to the following guidelines when using a pep talk to motivate athletes:

- *Make sure that your pep talk has a theme.* Expressing a specific, straightforward message is important. It could be about perseverance, poise, or points. You decide the subject, select the words, give an illustration to help them understand, and be sure they're attentive.
- *Eliminate distractions.* In the locker room, don't give the pep talk when they're dressing, listening to music, or adjusting their uniform or equipment. Athletes should be seated, relaxed, and quiet.

Ron Alvey/Shutterstock.com

Pep talks should be business-like in tone and format, where the coach expresses, as clearly and as briefly as possible, what awaits the athletes and what is expected of them.

- *Avoid gimmicks and impromptu pep talks.* Most of these are doomed to fail. And don't make promises (like to shave your head or run behind the bus), since such stunts lead more to amusement than motivation. For example, a Florida football coach staged a fake shooting of himself during a pep talk in the school cafeteria. After players fled in horror and three police cars raced to the school, he admitted that the stunt was "poorly contrived. What a gross mistake." That night his team lost the game 27-14. The coach explained, "Football demands so much physically, mentally, and spiritually; that was an attempt to motivate them to perform over their limits." The school superintendent disagreed: "It is my opinion that using a weapon of any sort—whether it's real or not—is totally inappropriate."

- *Allow others to give the pep talk.* There's no rule that says the coach must be the one to always give the pep talk. Community leaders, former athletes, popular teachers, or administrators can speak to the team before a competition or at practices. Even better, athletes can give each other pep talks, if the coach guides them correctly through that process.

- *Determine the best intensity level of the pep talk.* Getting athletes "psyched up" has its rewards and its faults. One athlete may need a high level of arousal, while another performs better when the motivation is more low key. Each athlete's arousal level needs to be evaluated; their personality, attitude, and maturity need to be assessed. If the athlete is introverted, less psyching is recommended, but not so low that they remain indifferent towards the competition.

For complex tasks or if additional competitions await the athlete (like in a tournament), then less arousal is often needed. Furthermore, a more experienced athlete often needs less of a pep talk.

To be sure, pep talks are a part of all sports, and most athletes, when they reminisce, can often still recall many years later their coaches' comments, good or bad, before an important competition. That said, the wise coach considers carefully much in advance the pep talk they want to give before a game or tournament. They then speak to the team in such a manner that the athletes compete in an inspired way.

Video the Athletes

68

Videotaping can serve as a great way to both instruct and motivate athletes. There are, of course, many ways to give feedback to athletes (ways that appeal to all learning styles) when evaluating their performances, but a favorite method is video. In this instance, you video the athletes' performance and then view this later to analyze their strong and weak points. Your positive commentary in this instance, can further add to their motivation.

Young athletes love watching themselves on television (or YouTube). Whether their performances were below or above expectation, they simply enjoy seeing themselves in action. You should exploit this and video them as much as possible—at selected practices, weekly competitions, a team project, etc. Then, let them view the video as soon as possible after the event, so they can get immediate feedback. You may decide to make a highlight video for the team or even each player, with dubbed in music and graphics to show at your awards program or a final team banquet. Either way, using this technology can do much to motivate today's athlete.

Videotaping can serve as a great way to both instruct and motivate athletes.

Haider Y. Abdulla/Shutterstock.com

69 Show Professionally Produced Videos

You can purchase either through catalogs or some sporting goods stores videos of outstanding college and professional athletes or teams in almost every sport. These highlight films are professionally produced and very motivational. Athletes can observe talented college and professional athletes in action, possibly hear commentary from them and their coaches, and enjoy a background soundtrack of popular music and professional announcers. You could also use these videos to talk about the great athletes who were very diligent and highly committed in their sport.

As you show videos of these individuals, comment on their intensity, enthusiasm, and perseverance. These videos, also found on YouTube, can both teach and inspire young athletes, and every coach should employ them at least once or twice during the season.

Videos can both teach and inspire young athletes, and every coach should employ them at least once or twice during the season.

Mail/Email a Newsletter

These types of correspondences are invaluable. They are the most effective way for any sports program or school group to advertise its achievements and communicate to athletes, fans, and other stakeholders. By profiling the team and your athletes' individual accomplishments, a newsletter can be a powerful tool for low-cost public relations. A newsletter promotes your program and generates motivation.

The parents, local media, school administrators, and fellow teachers all deserve to be informed about the team's progress through the season (and all school year in some cases). Newsletters update parents, fans, administration, and the community on individual and team results, new rules, and upcoming events, which, in turn, increases their interest in the program and builds your credibility and professional standing. Reading about themselves and the team in these newsletters keeps athletes motivated because you have presented them in a positive manner. You could also use a newsletter to convey special motivational messages.

No matter what type of newsletter you eventually design, you are conveying an important image to your athletes and the community (parents especially). Formats and styles of newsletters can vary, yet each should provide some common information, including the following:

- An introduction that grabs the readers' attention on the first page and keeps them reading. *Have our hearts recovered? Those nail-biting victories over Aurora and Newbury certainly caused the adrenaline to flow and the cheers to erupt. My kids, Your kids . . . <u>Our</u> kids were psyched and relentless. They demanded the victory, and they got it! Your presence and support really helped make it happen.*

maicasaa/Shutterstock.com

Newsletters update parents, fans, administration, and the community on individual and team results, new rules, and upcoming events, which, in turn, increases their interest in the program and builds your credibility and professional standing.

- Game and tournament results
- Dates and times of upcoming competitions
- Updates or announcements about important events or honors that involve the team or individual athletes for example—*The team finished as the Associated Press's number one rated school in Division III for the season, which was determined by the votes of coaches across the state. Tickets for the state basketball tournament are $25.00/packet and can be purchased from the athletic director.*
- Individual statistics
- Comments from assistant coaches and/or administrators, for example—*"I'm enjoying the opportunity to coach these young student-athletes, yet I caution them to be 'doers' and not 'talkers.' We cannot relax but continue to strive toward becoming the best we can be."*
- Inspirational quotes, for example—*"Courage is not how a man stands or falls, but how he gets back up again."* (from John L. Lewis).
- A trivia question, for example—*What athlete holds the record for most career tennis wins at our school?*
- Reminders related to dates and times of special events or the collection of equipment and uniforms
- Public thank you's to administrators and/or parents, for example—*Thanks to Mrs. Patricia Ranes, our principal, and Dr. Marc Crane, superintendent, for the dedicated support of our program. They remain constantly attentive to the needs of the coaching staff and showed a special understanding of our athletes. We owe our success in part to you.*

You could also use the newsletter to post an Athlete of the Week award winner, the players' academic honors, or your athletes' accomplishments in other sports. A colleague called his newsletter "Miluk's Minutes," in which he listed the significant details related to his program—tournament results, the date and location of a team picnic, fundraisers, and rules clarifications, along with an interesting trivia question and a famous quote to keep parents and fans informed and interested in his program.

Possibly one of your more artistic athletes can assist you in creating a unique and bold logo or masthead for your newsletter. You can also use colorful graphics, high-quality illustrations, and vivid photographs. Be sure the print is clear and easy to read. If you can establish a positive connection between yourself and the parents, your position in the school and community becomes more prominent, and your team itself becomes more popular and motivated. As before, effective and regular communication is the key. A newsletter can accomplish this for you.

Provide Awards 71

A varsity track athlete identifies his motivation as an athlete: "I enjoy playing sports with my friends, but I participate for the awards of trophies and medals." Sports psychologist Dr. Robert Weinberg surveyed junior and senior high school age athletes and discovered many were motivated by the extrinsic need to gain rewards. This segment focuses on the athlete's need for extrinsic motivation.

Awards can fulfill that need and do much to satisfy most athletes' desire for a tangible reward for their efforts. These weekly or monthly awards can be plaques, trophies, medals, certificates, T-shirts, ribbons, or patches for letter jackets, accompanied of course by a public address announcement the next day announcing the award winner.

Research by Andrew Hamilton and colleagues found "that the simultaneous presence of high extrinsic and high intrinsic motivation is likely to yield the most positive benefits for . . . athletes. However, it is critical that extrinsic motives are nurtured on a firm foundation of high intrinsic motivation. Without high intrinsic motivation, athletes are likely to drop out when they encounter problems, such as an injury, non-selection, or demotion." Hamilton also concluded that "the reward should be presented to an athlete in front of all potential recipients, with some emphasis placed on the prestige associated with it. Other popular ways of using token rewards include etching athletes' names on annual honors boards for their contributions or awarding a special item of clothing."

You may choose to give awards for the top performance at practice each week, for the top performance (not necessarily a victorious one) at the most recent competition, or for a display of outstanding sportsmanship or community service. Hamilton asserts, "the key aspect in using extrinsic rewards effectively is that they reinforce an athlete's sense of competence and self-worth."

Greg Shelley of the Janssen Sports Leadership Center, however, cautions coaches not to overuse awards or "incentives" during a season. "Incentives too can be effective for the short-term. Dangling the 'carrot' (e.g., playing time, money, trophies) is a strong motivator for many athletes, but these extrinsic means generally last for only a short time before the 'incentives' need [to be] increased or made more appealing. The less appealing the incentive, the less motivation one will generally show."

Whatever award you choose to use, be sure there is a concrete criteria attached to it. Overall, awards can do much to motivate many players.

72 Acknowledge Contributions

In this instance, it is essential to make sure that each athlete knows they are making a strong contribution to the program. Overall, to keep athletes motivated, the coach has to make them feel special as a member of the team. Their personal achievements have to be recognized and praised. They have to know that the coach cares about them personally and that they are making an important contribution to helping the team achieve its goals. It's also okay to brag about their accomplishments in the school and in the community.

Second, special acknowledgement of those athletes who are junior varsity or nonstarters is crucial. They are as important to any program as the superstars and should be treated with as much attention as the varsity. This strategy does much to develop their intrinsic motivation, as suggested by the research of Andrew Hamilton and his colleagues. Hamilton says, a "wealth of evidence . . . suggests that a focus on personal mastery and intrinsic motivation (enjoyment) brings the most positive motivation outcomes." Thus, in the case of marginal athletes, well-phrased compliments enhance their sense of belonging, self-esteem, and motivation.

It is essential to make sure that each athlete knows they are making a strong contribution to the program.

Stick Signs in Their Yards

In Chillicothe, Illinois, the mothers construct and paint signs to put in the front yards of each football player 9th through 12th grade. Since the school (Illinois Valley Central High School) nickname is "Grey Ghosts," they print in crimson letters "Home of a Grey Ghost FB Player" and the outline in gray of a ghost behind it on a 3' x 3' sign. In Bay Village, Ohio, the football players' signs are in the shape of football helmets. The player's number is in white on a blue helmet.

This type of motivation can work in any town and community. Moreover, a sign adds to a player's sense of team pride and recognition. It invites compliments, offers of good luck, and congratulations after competitions. Coaches, art students, student council members, parents, and pep clubs can all contribute to the design, construction, and distribution of these signs, which can do a lot to motivate athletes.

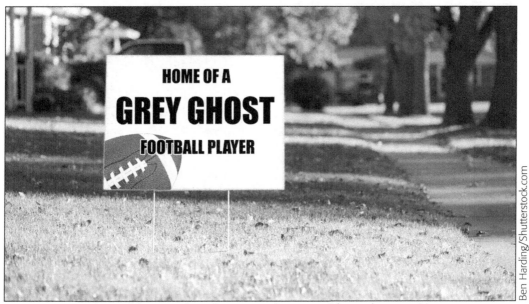

A sign adds to a player's sense of team pride and recognition.

74 Decorate Athletes' Lockers

In many schools, the cheerleaders or pep club decorate the lockers of every athlete during their season of competition. To the locker, they tape the player's number, school logo, possibly a picture and balloons, and good luck signs, along with colored crepe paper. Through the course of the season, decorations related to that week's upcoming contest (e.g., "Beat the Panthers!") are added. This brings each athlete team recognition, personal satisfaction, and individual motivation.

Decorating lockers can do much to motivate athletes, but be sure school administrators, custodians, and teachers are informed about your intent. If the cheerleaders are too busy, you can ask the student council, pep club, art club, or team managers to do this.

Decorating lockers can do much to motivate athletes.

Brocreative/Shutterstock.com

Expect Positive Outcomes   **75**

Expecting positive outcomes means you have confidence, and when you demonstrate confidence in yourself and your athletes, you discover the power of charisma. You don't have to be movie-star charming, but you do have to be direct and committed to expecting positive outcomes.

You can capitalize on the players' intrinsic motivation by challenging them to learn new techniques and predicting with enthusiasm they will master them. And if they fail to master them right away, show no concern or worry. In fact, tolerate those mistakes, since errors are natural to any learning process, especially if you expect a positive outcome. Work, then, to eliminate errors through drill sessions, instruction, and positive reinforcement. A junior high soccer player appreciates his coaches because "they don't let you quit, when they know you can do the job."

According to Domique Stasulli's article "How Coaches Contribute to Athletes' Motivation," "One of the best coaching skills is the ability to bring positive enthusiasm to athletes. A 2014 study found a positive correlation between athlete optimism and race times and an inverse relation to negativity." Inform athletes of Thomas Jefferson's comment: "Nothing can stop the man with the right mental attitude from achieving his goal; nothing on earth can help the man with the wrong mental attitude."

To be sure, the obstacles to positive outcomes are criticism and confrontations. No athlete or coach escapes some form of disapproval during their career. Yet, with effort, every coach can transform this negative energy into a positive, productive outcome. How?

- Anticipate problems before they reach the crisis stage.
- Maintain a professional demeanor, although others may be dominated by their emotions.
- Remain assertive, but not confrontational, when dealing with opposing points of view.
- Repair damaged relationships through compromise and cooperation.
- Recognize the differences between healthy and harmful anger in the players and show how to channel this emotion into effort, not antagonism.
- Confront difficult people and situations directly, without being intimidated or provoked.
- Be regularly accessible for others when a problem comes up.
- Communicate in a honest, straightforward way with athletes.
- Refuse to let any kind of criticism ruin your effectiveness as a coach.

76 Be Attentive and Provide Feedback

Being attentive to athletes means giving them appropriate feedback when necessary. First, what is appropriate feedback and second, how should this feedback be delivered?

Unfortunately, most coaches' feedback surfaces as criticism. The athlete, in turn, experiences, according to researcher Alexander Hamilton, "feelings of incompetence and a lack of connection between [their] behavior and the expected outcome. For example, a motivated athlete might be heard saying, 'I can't see the point in training any more—it just tires me out' or 'I just don't get any buzz out of competition whatsoever.' Such athletes exhibit a sense of helplessness and often require counselling, as they are highly prone to dropping out."

You certainly do not want the athlete to quit. Sara Robinson, MA, reminds coaches that "as a coach, you can encourage intrinsic motivation by helping athletes see their improvements, giving positive feedback that is related to skill development, and by having the athletes talk about what they did well and what they have been learning." Hamilton's additional research points to "tentative support for the proposition that focusing on personal mastery and self-referenced goals promotes intrinsic motivation to a greater degree than focusing on winning and demonstrating superiority over others."

How should a coach deliver feedback to an athlete to keep them motivated? This could occur through a private or team discussion about their progress, a critique of their techniques, or praise for their efforts. You could give your players weekly, possibly daily, notification of their development through posted charts or statistics.

You should also provide specific information about performances (practice or competition) to the players who have set their own training goals. This constant assessment (beyond generic commentary, for example, like "You did a nice job today" or "That was a good takedown") encourages athletes to set personal standards for their practice and, hence, the competition. Better, more specific compliments would be, "You never stopped hustling during practice today. You're setting a standard I'd like everyone to follow. Well done!" or "Your finish on your single leg was excellent. Do it that way all the time and no one will stop it." In fact, they should be given some indications of their improvement after each practice. That shows you are being attentive and keeps them motivated.

Sometimes, subordinates may feel uncertain about approaching you with their ideas or concerns. Don't be so wrapped up in your own agenda that you tune them out. Also, never ignore your athletes. This suggests you are apathetic and uncaring. This type of behavior lowers their morale and decreases their motivation. Instead, as often as possible, present opportunities for dialogues with other coaches and athletes and then listen attentively. Just listening with true interest and responding positively can do much to motivate young athletes.

Be a Counselor

Maybe this is a duty you would prefer not to accept, but to motivate today's athletes, you probably should always be ready to counsel them about their personal problems. This is crucial, since so many young athletes do not have the positive homelife we would like them to have. "I get motivated when I know the coach is concerned about every athlete on the team, from the best to the worst," says one high school football player. "A coach has to be like a second father who can teach you about sports and life."

"The coach we hire must have a solid value system, which places importance on kindness to others," says a high school principal. "The individual must show genuine care for athletes and know how to teach that attitude to them." This statement emphasizes the importance of coaches showing concern for the athletes' welfare and being attentive towards their personal needs. A high school baseball player adds: "It's important that the coach is more than a coach, he's a friend, too. He has to understand me and discipline me."

Being a counselor can refer simply to maintaining regular dialogues with players in situations other than practice that don't include nagging them about their schoolwork or their last competition. Build motivation by recognizing when others' personal problems are affecting their performance and assist them in eliminating those problems.

Once coaches accept this responsibility, they are more likely to increase the motivation of their athletes. The players and general public will come to admire them for their commitment and sincerity, their compassion and concern. Coaches who also act as counselors will probably enjoy a loyal following as well.

Being a counselor can refer simply to maintaining regular dialogues with players in situations other than practice that don't include nagging them about their schoolwork or their last competition.

Monkey Business Images/Shutterstock.com

78 Reduce the Athlete's Anxiety

How much does success depend on the athlete's physical skills and how much on their mental attitude to the sport? If you consider the players' psychological makeup, you are probably addressing their frustrations, worries, and self-esteem issues. Thus, to lessen athletes' anxieties, how much of a psychologist does a coach have to be?

You don't have to be Sigmund Freud. You do, however, have to be prepared to identify the emotional and psychological state of your players, especially in the ways they react to success and failure, if you want to keep them motivated.

Dominique Stasulli in the article "How Coaches Contribute to Athletes' Motivation" cites some key research in her article. "Stress is an important consideration in an athlete's overall well-being and can be inversely related to self-esteem. Coaching pressures often cause distress to those athletes who have an egocentric mindset… An ego-involved climate can endanger the athlete's self-esteem with constant social comparison and questions about their adequacy."

For some coaches, achievement is accompanied by stress and anxiety. As a winning coach, you may face the pressure of staying successful, of repeating a championship, of setting new standards of excellence. Though victory can be exhilarating, success can present a fresh set of problems.

It is the same for athletes who may feel pressure to recreate their achievements and win each time they compete, even if it is at the state tournament. Fans and/or parents may expect these accomplishments every season. Some athletes then find themselves struggling not to lose, rather than striving to win.

It is this stress that can weaken a player's effectiveness. Every week of any typical season, athletes can experience tension caused by conflicts with teammates and/or parents. Even their own competitive attitude can lead to anxiety, as they push themselves to win games or matches. In this kind of domain, disagreements are common, and confrontations are frequent. If they are not handled effectively, it is possible that the player's composure can collapse and their motivation suffers.

Many potentially successful performances are lost just prior to a game due to getting "psyched out," losing confidence, becoming unfocused, or experiencing something unexpected. The wise coach must prepare athletes to prepare for and cope with all potentially debilitating events.

What are the stress situations that can get in the way of success? Personal frustrations in school, arguments with family or friends, previous failures at a competition, and unfamiliar settings (e.g., five thousand fans at the district tournament vs. two hundred at a home game) are all typical stress-inducing situations. Dr. Jim Taylor cites that stress can "include the ability of the opponent and external factors, such as an 'away game' crowd, and weather, such as temperature, wind, and sun. You have no control over these factors."

Look first for symptoms associated with anxiety (e.g., doubt, anger, frustration, negativity, regrets, and even poor health). Athletes may leave conflicts unresolved and sometimes overreact to challenges. They may complain of stomach cramps and loss of appetite, lose concentration, withdraw from others, talk too often about the season being over, or overreact to minor problems. If they can eliminate their own self-destructive behaviors and emotional surges, they can become better performers in competitions.

Some athletes, when confronting stress, choose to avoid it by quitting. Several sports psychologists call this "burnout." Other terminology is "mental fatigue" and "getting stressed out."

What is it, therefore, that you can do to turn worry into winning and tension into triumph? Coaches need some lessons on the psychology of pressure and the power of positive thinking to keep their athletes motivated.

Feeling pressure is, in effect, a complaint about a problem. Whether the goal is to master a baton handoff for a relay or sink two foul shots, an athlete may feel there's *something* wrong, and they can't succeed. Suddenly, more than one obstacle exists: the actual physical challenge and the anxiety.

Most individuals try to hide their anxiety, but this is the wrong way to go. Although unpleasant, all this worry must be talked about and brought out into the open. The pressure, even the feeling of fear, has to be acknowledged. Stress can't be ignored.

Understanding pressure means dealing with anxiety, especially the anxiety of an uncertain outcome. For too many athletes, their imaginations more often dramatize failure rather than success. Their opponents become stronger than they really are, and their own weaknesses are magnified.

Stress cannot be overcome with emotion. Disgust, anger, or rage do nothing to improve skills or smarts. Therefore, it is important for you to explain that every competition involves a degree of uncertainty. This shouldn't be feared; it should be enjoyed. Winning in sports is especially exciting when it occurs against an opponent who possesses equal or greater ability. Athletes and coaches should exert faith in their abilities, not fury.

Roy Campanella achieved great success as a major league baseball player and coach. He also confronted his paralysis with the same dynamic attitude. He gives excellent advice: "When you're in a slump, you don't feel sorry for yourself. That's when you have to try harder. You have to have faith, hope, and conviction that you can lick it . . . You just have to be mentally tough."

Often, an essential element to mental preparation is to remove the tension associated with taking a risk. The coach can create problem scenarios in practice— "We're losing by one goal, we have the puck by our net, and there are only thirty seconds to go in the final period. What should we do?"—and invite players to solve them, encouraging them to be unafraid to take the risk that could result in victory.

The following are 10 techniques that coaches can use with their athletes to help them defeat anxiety and stay motivated:

- Direct them to a coach, fellow athlete, family member, clergyman, or teacher to help talk out the problem.
- Establish a means of relaxation that includes some form of meditation, deep breaths, and a warmup that leaves them relaxed and alert.
- Explain instructions carefully, which helps to eliminate any uncertainties about what is expected or demanded especially before a game.
- Make players familiar with what may be unfamiliar to them (e.g.., play loud music in practice to simulate crowd noise).
- Demand that they always stay under control and concentrate during a competition.
- Remind them about what they should and should not eat (nutrition).
- Be sure they are knowledgeable about any information associated with that competition (for example, if it is a double-elimination or single-elimination tournament).
- Discuss their expectations and share the coaches' expectations.
- Demand they listen to coaches, captains, and officials.
- Keep reminding them they are strong, worthy competitors who *can* succeed.

In truth, virtually all athletes perceive competitions as threatening because there is always a possibility of defeat. It is the unexpected that prompts stress to occur for most athletes.

Dr. Martin Stein, a professor of pediatrics at the University of California-San Diego School of Medicine, clarifies that "the experience of tension or stress is a normal aspect of development. It's a part of every child's life, from infancy to adolescence." Coaches shouldn't feel hesitant about "taking the first steps to discuss a problem with school staff—nurses, teachers, counselors, or support workers—and the child's family." Stein offers two more strategies: teach in creative ways and be ready to communicate. Have athletes concentrate on tasks, not outcomes.

A successful coach/athlete relationship requires a balance of respect, confidence, and comfort. Coaches must create an atmosphere that lessens the athletes' stress and allows them to feel a sense of control. Any sports season is a journey, sometimes a long one, for athletes who undoubtedly will encounter obstacles and difficulties. Coaches, therefore, must be prepared to guide them through this.

Counteract Peer Pressure

Another type of stress that can hinder motivation is the pressure athletes receive from their peers. For example, they may be pressured to break training rules, to skip practice, to participate in underage drinking, or to use illegal drugs. Satisfying the needs of friends is a strong motivator for most young people, and today's coaches must work hard to prevent their athletes from becoming victims of peer pressure, which preys upon their moods and emotions. Your athletes can better deal with peer pressure if you prepare them ahead of time, first, to recognize and, second, to resist it.

Keep in mind that you cannot pick the athletes' friends for them, and you cannot order them to abandon certain friends, regardless of your worries about their backgrounds or intents. Approach them instead with questions: How do your friends support you as an athlete? What are they doing to help you succeed? How often do they attend your competitions? Do they encourage or discourage you from breaking training rules? What are their attitudes toward this team and the coaches?

Avoid lecturing. They may tune you out or, worse, challenge your authority. The goal is to help athletes make the right decision when faced with peer pressure, and posing questions and possibly offering some personal anecdotes from your own life when you confronted peer pressure are stronger ways to get athletes thinking about the correct choice to make.

You might also role play some scenarios that involve peer pressure as in "What would you do if . . .?" Emphasize the mental toughness they have as athletes and boost their emotional self-esteem when their responses to the role play are appropriate. Also, encourage teammates to support each other, that the team as "family" can help everyone deal with any type of peer pressure.

When you show your athletes, through questions and anecdotes, that you understand peer pressure and then express faith that they can deal with it successfully on their own, you increase their personal levels of confidence in both you and themselves. Remind your players to take pride in their athletic achievements and clarify their strong points as athletes; this can assist them in overcoming peer pressure from outside the program. And finally, when you model ways to react to peer pressure, you prepare them ahead of time to handle it. The unfortunate reality is that most kids will confront peer pressure almost daily, so the wise coach must be ready to deal with it frequently to keep athletes motivated.

80 Take Pictures

If it is true that a picture is worth a thousand words, then it makes sense that pictures can motivate athletes in ways that speeches can't. Have either a professional or an amateur (a parent?) photographer take pictures of your athletes at practice, in competitions, and during any training session and then post them in display cases and in classrooms. You may even place them on the windows or doors of community businesses. Be sure captions accompany the pictures identifying the athletes' names and the situation (for example, Jenny Jones and Sally Smith leap for a rebound against Amherst High School).

Arrange for the school newspaper and yearbook to publish pictures of your players. With today's digital cameras this is easily accomplished. You can request managers, statisticians, or the spirit club to complete a scrapbook for each senior athlete, who then receives it at an awards program at the end of the season.

You can also take pictures of your varsity and the junior varsity "Player of the Week," and post them in a display case or on a locker room bulletin board. Update these as often as possible because photographs can have a strong influence on your players' motivation.

Pictures can motivate athletes in ways that speeches can't.

Motivation is not restricted to the practice room, the field, or the gym. Though some coaches (and many administrators) may worry about supervision, don't be hesitant about taking your team out together. Possibilities in this instance include dinner, a movie, a school play, another sporting contest, a college game, or an arcade.

The point is to use this experience to build positive relationships with the athletes and to establish a rapport with them. You must be the catalyst for this relationship-building process. With rapport comes acceptance of you and the program, and it follows then that everyone directly involved with the program can more easily and readily accept the validity and value of the team's objectives. Planning this event can take, to be sure, considerable time and effort, but the ultimate reward is an increase in your players' motivation and buy-in into your program.

Alena Haurylik/Shutterstock.com

Motivation is not restricted to the practice room, the field, or the gym.

82   Plan a Retreat

Though you and your administration may worry about supervision in this instance, team unity, friendship, and motivation are developed through this retreat activity. You can arrange this get-away for any season of the year, depending on your personal schedule and goals. In the summer, some coaches take their teams camping and canoeing, while others have a picnic and softball game. One coach invited the entire team to his home during the season for a sleepover that involved video games, pool, ping pong, pizza, and cards.

Clearly, a strong sense of fellowship can be established within the team, and the kids and the coaches can strengthen their rapport. When arranging this activity, be sure parents and administrators are clearly informed about all plans. An effectively organized retreat can certainly motivate many athletes.

Team unity, friendship, and motivation can be developed through a retreat activity.

lassedesignen/Shutterstock.com

Text/Phone/Tweet/Email Athletes

Cell phones and email have transformed the way individuals communicate these days, and wise coaches should take advantage of them to motivate their athletes. You can phone and email athletes to praise, thank, or acknowledge them for their performances in practice or games. Use a text, tweet, or email to compliment effort in practice or to praise a performance (i.e., "I like your intensity in practice. That kind of effort will help you win this weekend" or "Your times are getting quicker. That's why you've won the last four swim meets").

Be sure that your statements are always affirmative and brief. You can talk at length on the phone, if time permits, and if there's much to say, but avoid taking up too much of the athlete's personal time away from school. Most often, a succinct but significant message is more motivating than a longer one.

Because cell phones and email have transformed the way individuals communicate these days, wise coaches should take advantage of them to motivate their athletes.

84 Visit Athletes at Their Homes

By going to the homes of athletes and their families, you demonstrate a commitment to their lives beyond the field, court, rink, or mat. "It's important that the coach is more than a coach," says a middle school wrestler. "He has to understand me." Robert Kanaby, former Executive Director of the National Federation of State High School Associations, tells coaches: "You just don't walk away when the game is won or lost. There's a responsibility that carries itself into the locker room, into the school bus, and right on down the line."

Therefore, you should not be hesitant about visiting and talking to your players at their homes. In fact, you should maintain regular dialogues with players in situations other than practice that don't include schoolwork or the sport. Such a visit can strengthen your rapport with the player and their family, as well as increase their motivation.

By going to the homes of athletes and their families, coaches demonstrate a commitment to their lives beyond the field, court, rink, or mat.

shurkin_son/Shutterstock.com

Send Cards and Letters **85**

Writing a personal note to an athlete can be time-consuming, but it is another effective method for motivating them. Such notes can include praise for a past performance, appreciation for their hard work, and/or acknowledgment of a special contribution they've made to the program. Avoid dealing with comments on skills or techniques; just focus on praise and compliments.

These can be inspirational messages, birthday cards, advice letters, congratulatory letters, or an invitation to join the program (see Figures 85-1 and 85-2). In any correspondence, you can be personal but not pushy. In addition, subsequently be sure to check that the athlete did in reality, receive whatever message you sent.

Dear Greg:

Watching you on the football field this fall convinces me you have the skills and the stamina to be a successful wrestler. I would bet that your hard-hitting style of play at linebacker is a key reason our team's defense is so highly ranked in the conference. I think your abilities can only get better if you compete on the wrestling team this season.

Sure, it might be tough at first, but if you're not afraid of challenges and like one-on-one competition where you don't have to depend on an entire team to make the "big play," then wrestling is the sport for you. Talk to some of the guys who are on the team and ask them about it. I'm certain they'd like to see you join.

I want to see you on the mats this winter, but for now, keep up the good work on the football field. Good luck in your game against _____ High School.

Sincerely,

Figure 85-1. An example of a personal note to an athlete

Dear _____

You really showed improvement this past season, and the coaches often talked about your hustle and enthusiasm. You really made the most of your talent and abilities, and we are eager to see even more improvement next year. We have a lot of confidence in you.

Whatever you lack in experience can be made up with lots of desire, extra work, and perseverance. Confidence comes with preparation. So let's start preparing.

Preparing for success—yours and the team's!

All the best,

Figure 85-2. An example of a personal note to an athlete

Use Social Media

86

Instagram, Facebook, and Twitter are the current social connections of many adolescents' daily lives. Therefore, a wise coach should take advantage of social media to motivate athletes. Through Instagram messages and pictures, Facebook posts, and weekly tweets, coaches can send messages of inspiration, congratulations, and accolades; all of these can be motivational. Indeed, the power of social media and its influence on relationships, especially between peers, should not be overlooked.

Strong relationships themselves are motivational. A study by Richard Rychman of the University of Maine in 1992 identified two key reasons for female teens to participate in sports: (1) to make new friends and (2) to continue current friendships. A clear conclusion is the importance of peer relations, social interactions, and regular reassurances required by beginner athletes, both male and female, to feel motivated to participate. Attentive coaches can employ Facebook, Twitter, and Instagram to communicate to their athletes and parents regarding team results, team social events, or upcoming competitions, along with messages of encouragement and support.

Coaches' social media messages can praise, thank, or acknowledge athletes for their performances in practice or games. Be sure that your statements are always affirmative and brief, given that most often, a succinct message is more motivating than a longer one. Athletes will work harder (and longer) for someone they know genuinely believes in them, cares about them, and is committed to helping them achieve their potential. At the heart of this motivational strategy is the quality of the coach-athlete relationship. Social media can accomplish this.

Coaches who use social media correctly can also gain support from parents and community members who can, in turn, support and motivate athletes. These adults can be regularly updated about the progress of the team and individual players. Social media messages promote open communication among all stakeholders in the athletic program, provide positive reinforcement and encouragement for athletes, and demonstrate a coach's concern and enthusiasm. They are the most effective way for any sports program or school group to advertise its achievements and communicate to its athletes and fans in a timely way. By profiling the team and the athletes' individual accomplishments, social media outlets can be a powerful tool for low-cost public relations.

Another social media outlet is YouTube. Note: Warning: If you decide to post videos of your athletes on YouTube, employ this motivational strategy only after obtaining written approval from both the athletes' parents and your school administration. The previous rash of Harlem Shake and Gangnam Style videos performed by various high school (including my sons' high school varsity baseball team) and college teams inspired a new approach to the use of YouTube in athletics. Indeed, YouTube clips can serve as a creative way to motivate athletes and, in turn, their classmates and possibly community members. With YouTube, every athlete can get their fifteen minutes of fame and recognition, which can add to their motivation while they develop team camaraderie.

Sharing the tweets and YouTube highlights of both professional and other amateur players can also motivate young athletes. As you share the tweets and videos of these individuals, comment on the athletes' intensity, enthusiasm, and perseverance as they train and compete. Your athletes can observe talented college and professional athletes in action, possibly hear commentary from them and their coaches, and enjoy a background soundtrack of popular music and professional announcers. You could also use these videos to talk about the great athletes who are highly committed. These social media options can both teach and inspire young athletes, and every coach should employ them at least several times during the season.

I suspect most young athletes would probably love watching themselves on the Internet, whether their performances were below or above expectation. They simply enjoy seeing themselves in action. Coaches can exploit this factor and, as a result, video their players as much as possible—during selected practices, at weekly competitions, even at a team function. Using social media can do much to motivate today's athlete.

In closing, if you can make a positive connection between yourself, the athletes, and the parents, your position in the school and community becomes more prominent, and your team itself, becomes more popular and motivated. The effective use of social media can make this happen.

Sharing the tweets and YouTube highlights of both professional and other amateur players can also motivate young athletes.

Host a "Parents' Night" Contest

87

A "Parents' Night" event is typically near the middle or end of the season, where players are introduced with their parents/guardians to the crowd in the bleachers. In this instance, prior to the competition, each player is escorted by their parent/guardians into the gym or onto the field as the announcer introduces them. An added highlight would be for each athlete to present their mother with a single flower and their father with a team T-shirt. This traditional and important event can be used to motivate both the players and their parents.

Keep in mind that some athletes may not have a mother or father; a grandparent, older sibling, or other relative may be their guardian. Furthermore, be sure all names are announced correctly and respectfully.

A "Parents' Night" event is typically near the middle or end of the season, where players are introduced with their parents/guardians to the crowd.

Lopolo/Shutterstock.com

88 Persist

Cathy Rigby, an Olympic gymnast in 1968, says "All athletes . . . have times when everything seems to go wrong . . . I found that at those times, I would push myself the hardest . . . You can accomplish anything if you're persistent enough."

The persistence to continue motivating athletes must involve the energy of the entire coaching staff. The head coach must assemble a staff where everyone supports each other and shares the same vision for the program. Although these individuals may possess different personalities, everyone must respect each other, deal cooperatively with challenges and problems, and assist the head coach in a persistent manner to motivate all athletes.

Furthermore, as the head coach, you must constantly present yourself as a leader and a role model. You should always try to improve your ability as a leader and boost your staff's enthusiasm. You must be prepared, though, to deal with tardiness, conflicts, and emotions. Overall, your style of leadership must be consistent and confident. Present an image of calm self-confidence. People, especially athletes, are motivated by leaders who appear strong, positive, and relaxed even during difficult situations.

The bottom line? Maintaining this image and high level of motivation takes persistence. This means you keep finding ways to appeal to your athletes' intrinsic need to do their best, their extrinsic need to gain rewards, and their personal reasons for enjoying competitions. As you do, be attentive to the needs of all your athletes and be sure that everyone is headed in the same direction.

The persistence to continue motivating athletes must involve the energy of the entire coaching staff.

Teach Commitment **89**

Let's take for granted that the greater the commitment by the athlete, the deeper their motivation. And let's assume that if you improve the athlete's commitment you can increase their motivation. But how can you teach athletes to become more committed to the team and the program?

First, you have to recognize that each athlete begins the season with a different level of commitment, a different reason for competing, and a different relationship with the coaching staff. Therefore, discover how committed each athlete is, define the level of commitment you feel is necessary for individual and team success, and, consequently, work to improve the athletes' commitment.

How? Try a private conversation with the athlete to learn how committed they are. It is best to do this before the season even begins, possibly during a free period at school or over the telephone. If you cannot accomplish it then, be sure to talk to the athlete before or after practice during the first week of the season. Ask the athlete: "What are you willing *to do* this year to make yourself and the team successful?"

Don't get upset or dismayed if their answers aren't dynamic descriptions of the great sacrifices they plan to make. Indeed, many players, especially younger ones, may respond with, "I don't know." You probably will be the first coach ever to ask them this. That is when you need to define commitment for them. Explain that committed athletes exhibit the following traits:

- Do not break training rules.
- Are goal-oriented (both team and individual).
- Are punctual for practices, meetings, and games.
- Attend all practices.
- Maintain enthusiasms and intensity during practice.
- Encourage their teammates.
- Enjoy challenges and work hard to accomplish them.
- Are dedicated and reliable.
- Are coachable and cooperative.
- Are responsible students in the classroom.

When you discuss commitment with athletes, it is best to point out an athlete who demonstrates these characteristics as a model. You can also offer an example of a previous player on the team who exemplified commitment (and motivation). Often, the committed athlete arrives early and stays late, maintains a positive attitude especially during a crisis, and anticipates success, not failure, before competitions.

You can even use a chart on a chalk board to simplify the teaching of commitment:

1-----2-----3-----4-----5-----6-----7-----8-----9-----10

Low Level   Average Level   High Level

The use of numbers can sometimes clarify commitment (and motivation) for kids, just as they would recognize the impact in a car that 80 MPH has as opposed to 40 MPH.

Athletes with low levels (1-3) typically arrive one minute before practice begins and leave one second after you've dismissed them. They may not show much aggressiveness in competitions or much emotion about success or failure.

Their lack of commitment need not be criticized. In time, they can be motivated to work toward higher levels. "An effective coach for me," says one a varsity athlete, "pushes me to the limit. It's someone who is dedicated, who gives you encouragement, but also who pushes you to the next level."

Identifying players with average levels of commitment (4-7) can be frustrating for a coach. Often, these athletes are uncertain whether they should do more or less. They give medium effort at practice and have average success at competitions. They always listen to the coach at practice but may lose their focus at a crucial moment in a contest.

Once again, hold off on the criticism. Initially, teach them how intensifying their commitment can benefit both the team and themselves. This kind of sacrifice doesn't happen easily. You need to develop a sound relationship with each individual both on and off the field, mat, rink, or court. If disagreements and questions occur, it's essential that they not only respect and trust your judgments, but also know you're very interested in them as individuals.

What kind of athlete matches up to numbers 8-10? This athlete practices hard after school and then runs at night. They are eager to learn and love to compete. The coach may see this athlete be the first to congratulate or console a teammate after a game. This type of athlete never complains no matter what the circumstances.

Note: you cannot judge commitment by wins and losses, and commitment is truly characterized by actions, not by talk. It may be appealing to hear an athlete say, "I am committed to being a state champion" but a better statement would be, "I am committed to *practicing and competing* like a state champion."

Commitment surfaces in what the athlete is willing *to do*. A statement like "I plan to give it all I've got" does little to indicate commitment. Better statements would be like the following ones from athletes in various sports, that clarify the actions, attitude, and motivation necessary for high level commitment:

- "I am committed to practice with intensity and alertness."
- "I am committed to learning all I can as a wrestler, following the coach's directions, and always making weight so the team doesn't have to forfeit."
- "I'm committed to practicing, learning, and acting like a state gymnastics champion."

As the season progresses, give an informal weekly progress report to each athlete where you discuss your observations of his commitment (see Figure 89-1). Review the chart, if necessary: "It looks like you're operating around #6, Jenny. Let's try to get to #8 tomorrow and #10 by match day. I know you have the ability, and I have confidence in you."

You may begin by discussing effective vs. ineffective statements of commitment, and then help players verbalize their commitment in terms of what they will do, not what they want to have happen. Again, don't become discouraged if you find that the younger athletes may not be willing to do very much. For these kids, engage them in making a single commitment like, for example, increasing their total pushups in a single practice from 50 to 100, then 150.

Finally, and most importantly, *you* must always demonstrate commitment in the 9-10 range. You should be the model that the kids can imitate. And point out to them how the team has succeeded or improved because of their commitment. It is hoped that in time your, athletes will realize the benefits of being committed.

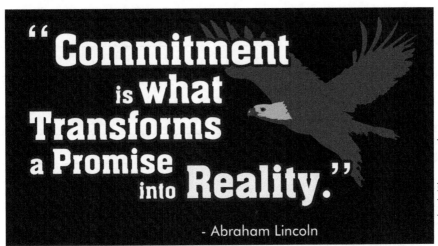

w3Mahesh/Shutterstock.com

Coaches have to recognize that each athlete begins the season with a different level of commitment, a different reason for competing, and a different relationship with the coaching staff.

Dr. Jim Taylor tells athletes, "Once you've made your [commitment], you must dedicate yourself to it. If your decision is to become the best athlete you can be, then this last step, dedication, will determine whether you have prime motivation. Your decision to be your best and your dedication to your sport must be top priorities. Only by being completely [committed] to your direction and decision will you ensure that you have prime motivation."

WEEKLY PROGRESS REPORT

Name _____   Date _____

The following is your rating in each category measuring your level of commitment this past week with *10* indicating a high mark and *1* indicating the lowest mark. It should be your goal to improve in each category each week.

Criteria	Rating (10-1)	Coaches' Comments
Mental Attitude	_____	_____
Dedication and Determination	_____	_____
Strength Work	_____	_____
Physical Conditioning	_____	_____
Cooperation With Others	_____	_____
Competitiveness	_____	_____
Enthusiasm and Motivation	_____	_____
Focus and Learning	_____	_____
AVERAGE SCORE	_____	_____

Figure 89-1. An example of a commitment progress report

Criticize Carefully

90

Given that criticism can have a damaging effect on motivation, when critiquing athletes either formally or informally, begin by having them do a self-evaluation. This precludes any defensive behavior on their part and helps maintain their motivation.

Begin by posing questions, for example: "What went wrong when you approached the first hurdle?" or "Why didn't that passing play work that time?" or "How can we improve our dribbling?" Then insist your athletes give you plain, honest feedback. Admit you don't have all the answers and be open to change. Accepting their responses as valid helps build their self-esteem and motivation.

Next, empathize with your athletes. Keep in mind that physical coordination, attention span, and experience levels vary from person to person, especially in younger athletes. Imagine yourself in their shoes before offering a criticism or complaint.

Finally, provide multiple opportunities to correct mistakes. Your athletes will probably appreciate your patience and feel less tension to make corrections immediately. And when they have made the proper corrections, praise them accordingly. This method appeals to their intrinsic motivation. Research from Andrew Hamilton and other psychologists suggests that this "[i]ntrinsic motivation comes from within, is fully self-determined and characterized by interest in, and enjoyment derived from, sports participation. There are three types of intrinsic motivation, namely intrinsic motivation to know, intrinsic motivation to accomplish and intrinsic motivation to experience stimulation. Intrinsic motivation is considered to be the healthiest type of motivation and reflects an athlete's motivation to perform an activity simply for the reward inherent in their participation."

Sara Robinson, writing for the National Alliance for Youth Sports, echoes this emphasis on intrinsic motivation. "While both internal and external factors can help to increase motivation, research has shown that helping to enhance intrinsic motivation is the best choice when it comes to long-term motivation. This makes sense: an athlete who is generally motivated because the game is fun and likes seeing themselves improve may be more likely to persist longer than an athlete who plays primarily to win games and get awards. Keep in mind that wanting to win and beat others is fine, but when these extrinsic factors are the only motivators, we run the risk of the athlete losing motivation, and potentially leaving the sport."

Be sure players recognize the reasons for any criticism. Most often, a quick explanation—"You need to do it this way because . . ." or "Here's why it's important to do it this way"—can accomplish that. When they accept the reasons, they are more willing to take on the responsibility for correcting a mistake, for overcoming their limitations, for improving their skills. An ultimate outcome is for them to take on the responsibility for their own success and/or defeat in competition.

The athletes who accept this kind of responsibility come to see instruction as an opportunity to eliminate a weakness and improve performance (intrinsic motivation). After recognizing the importance of mastering a certain skill, they are eager to test themselves at it even if it isn't easily accomplished. They show more effort and listen more closely. They are also more motivated.

The wise coach, therefore, prefaces instruction and criticism by first opening with questions to get the athlete mentally engaged before discussing the reasons for correcting the error. The coach then provokes the athletes' sense of personal motivation by challenging them to persevere beyond their initial mistakes and to surpass their limitations.

Simply, coaching is teaching, and the best coaches are often the best teachers. Because criticism is often part of the learning process, be sure to make it constructive criticism and be selective in using it. If you truly care about the athletes' self-motivation and personal achievement, avoid repeating criticism. Moreover, compliment their personal efforts more than you criticize their public mistakes.

Because criticism is often part of the learning process, be sure to make it constructive criticism and be selective in using it.

Show Your Mail

91

Showing your athletes the positive correspondences you get from college or opposing coaches can add tremendous credibility for you and your program and, in turn, some motivation for them to succeed on the field, court, rink, or mat. Share with your athletes any written praise the team receives from opposing coaches (make copies if necessary), school administrators, internal or external stakeholders (fans, parents), or colleagues. You should also or ask team captains to read these letters out loud. Do the same for the emails, the cards, and the direct mail you receive. Read these complimentary correspondences at the beginning of practice during announcements, when the athletes are probably most attentive and eager to listen.

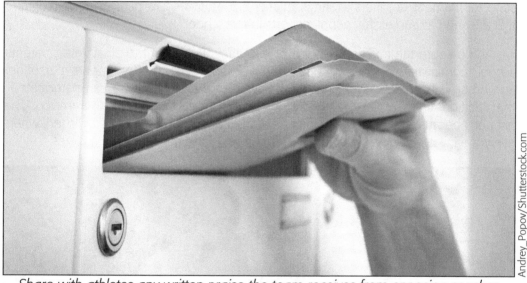

Andrey_Popov/Shutterstock.com

Share with athletes any written praise the team receives from opposing coaches (make copies if necessary), school administrators, internal or external stakeholders (fans, parents), or colleagues.

Honor Traditions

If you are a veteran coach, you probably have been honoring one tradition or another for years. Maybe, it is an annual spaghetti dinner in the preseason or distributing a special award at the post-season awards program. Novice coaches, however, either need to adopt or create special traditions associated with their teams. Whatever your situation, establishing and honoring a team tradition can be important to the overall morale and motivation of athletes.

Traditions can certainly add credibility to any program (for example, having an alumni or hall of fame game, in which you honor former athletes) and can suggest a repetition of success (for instance, a ceremony is held every year for either regional or state tournament qualifiers). Many athletes are motivated to participate in programs that are seen as successful, popular sports in the school.

And be sure the tradition is not a private affair. Publicize it to all athletes, parents, school administrators, fellow coaches, community members, support personnel, and other stakeholders. When the entire school (and community) can participate in the tradition, team achievement and personal accomplishment are maximized. This happens because a supportive, tradition-oriented network has been established, where everyone involved in the program seeks to benefit (and motivate) the athletes.

n_defender/Shutterstock.com

Establishing and honoring a team tradition can be important to the overall morale and motivation of athletes.

Host a Tournament

Encourage your administration to host one tournament—either at the varsity, junior varsity, freshmen, or middle school level—to expose (both) the student body to the excitement of the sport and (2) the players to the excitement of receiving individual awards in front of a large, mostly home-based crowd. A tournament can also be advantageous to the booster club, which can use a weekend tournament to obtain revenues by selling food, beverages, and candy at a concession stand. One local school hosts their "Mighty Mite" wrestling tournament in order "to bring wrestlers, coaches, fans, and parents together in a positive money maker."

In Ohio, tournaments are in operation almost every weekend of the school year—fall, winter, and spring. This is probably duplicated in many states. Competing for trophies, plaques, medals, or ribbons appeals to many athletes' extrinsic motivation, and placing in a tournament can provide the opportunity for them to receive such awards. Or you may decide to attend another school's tournament, and if so, you should allow the athletes and their parents to decide the tournament(s) where they wish to compete. Be ready to provide forms, directions, and information about these tournaments to school personnel, fans, and parents.

Encourage athletes to participate in post-season tournaments as well (sports like wrestling, volleyball, track, golf, tennis, basketball, and travel baseball and softball make this possible in the summer in many states). These events, scheduled annually and usually open to athletes of all ages, enable athletes to compete in the off-season at the local, state, regional, and national level and to improve their skills. The experience can do much to enhance their self-confidence for the next season and maintain the high level of motivation they have for that sport.

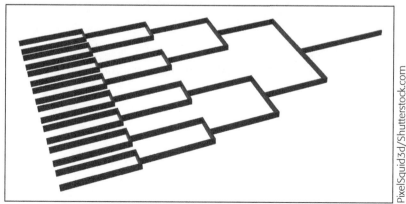

PixelSquid3d/Shutterstock.com

In many states, tournaments are in operation almost every weekend of the school year—fall, winter, and spring.

94 Use Audiobooks

Since so many athletes these days have headphones, earbuds, and music players, using audiobooks from motivational speakers offers another way to motivate them. Consider purchasing or borrowing from the school's or local library, the audiobooks produced by noted speakers like Anthony Robbins ("Personal Power"), Jeff Keller, Jack Canfield, Wayne Dyer, or Zig Zigler and then distributing them one at a time to your athletes. You may even distribute them to players as they travel with you on a long bus ride or as they sit in the bleachers at a tournament. Be selective and preview the content yourself first, so you know the message is one you want your players to hear. You can also go online to www.audiomotivation.com to investigate more audiobooks to use to motivate your athletes.

Using audiobooks from motivational speakers offers another way to motivate athletes.

Nor Gal/Shutterstock.com

The school's English teachers will certainly support you here. When you prompt athletes to read books that deal with positive thinking and motivation, you not only use an effective motivational tool, you also improve their reading skills (academics). These books could also be biographies of people who became successful due to their own perseverance and effort, other nonfiction books about motivation and success, or even novels that deal in a positive way with sports or teams. Get the books yourself and distribute them one at a time to your athletes or simply offer the titles to them and recommend they go to the library on their own. You might, in fact, suggest they read one or more of the following:

- *Great Book of Inspiring Quotations* by Peter Klavora
- *Another 1001 Motivational Messages and Quotes* by Bruce Brown.
- *The Edge* by Howard Ferguson
- *Purpose Lies Within: A Motivational Book for the Heart and Soul* by Kimberly Phillips, et. al.
- *Great Motivation Secrets of Great Leaders* by John Baldoni
- *Motivation and Goal Setting* by Jim Cairo
- *Chicken Soup for the Teenage Soul* by Jack Canfield

There are, of course, many more titles available, and a search through your library catalog, a bookstore, or on Amazon.com can identify them for you. You might even check out several to read yourself and come up with more ways to motivate players. For example, check out and read *The Big Book of Motivation Games* by Robert Epstein.

Some athletes may read only part of the book before returning it to you, but even a single story or quote from that book could make an impact. Reading is a private experience and gives you, as the coach, another way to motivate athletes away from the practice area and their teammates. Your more introverted players may appreciate this. Plus, this type of motivation will appeal to fellow teachers, administrators, and parents.

iunewind/Shutterstock.com

96 Win Games

There is no fault in wanting to win. It is natural, even beneficial in order to satisfy competitive urges, to strive to win in competition. All coaches work to achieve championships for their teams and themselves. In fact, athletic administrators expect that they try to do so. Such expectations can give players purpose, direction, and motivation.

Vince Lombardi said: "It is a reality of life that men are competitive, and the most competitive games draw the most competitive men. That's why they are here—to compete. The object is to win fairly, squarely, by the rules—but to win." Charlie Brown said: "Winning ain't everything, but losing is nothing."

Winning is definitely more fun than losing, and celebrations after victories do much for players' self-esteem and motivation. Your challenge, as a coach, is to avoid attaching so much importance to wins and losses that they become the basic tenant for judging the athletic program. Often, this can debilitate your players' motivation.

There is, indeed, no joy in losing. A loss in any form can be crushing, but in athletics, rarely is it the end. Learning how to handle a setback, a hardship, or a loss prepares young people for the difficulties outside athletics. "As teachers and coaches, we must remember that when mere winning is our only goal, we are doomed to disappointment and failure. But when our goal is to try to win, when our focus is on preparation and sacrifice and effort, instead of on numbers on a scoreboard, then we will never lose," says Mike Krzyzewski, Duke University basketball coach.

It is not uncommon for a coach, especially a very competitive one, to be tempted to abandon their principles because of the pressure to win. But this ultimately can work against their efforts to motivate athletes and maintain employment. "We do not want a coach who wants to win at all cost," says Louis Pronga, former athletic director at Illinois Valley Central High School. "The coach should be a good role model, who teaches by example. Winning is not a factor in how we hire a coach. It's more important that we get someone who has professional ethics and commitment. Sports are only one part of the educational process." Former MLB relief pitcher and baseball announcer Tug McGraw says, "Always accept that if you're willing to enjoy winning, you must bear the burden of occasional losses as well."

Sports gives young people an opportunity to strive for excellence, to risk losing in order to learn, and to grow into successful persons. Winning should not be the end of their goal-setting, it should be only the beginning.

Furthermore, creating the circumstances that make winning happen is certainly challenging and ongoing. Each season may require new strategies, but the experienced coach realizes this. Each season means you have a new team, seniors have graduated, newcomers have joined, a fresh group to teach to win. Just be careful not to sabotage your success by being overconfident or over-estimating your team's strengths or to base achievement on any one game.

When coaches focus their program on the number of wins produced by the season's end, they are setting themselves up to ride an emotional rollercoaster. That's the bad news. The good news is that you don't have to buy a ticket. If you get too pumped up about winning and too depressed about losing, you can find yourself riding the gut-wrenching peaks and valleys of a rollercoaster track. This not only can be an emotional nightmare, it's also unhealthy, especially if athletes notice. That observation could lessen their motivation.

One high school athlete comments, "I like a coach who always pushes his team to their full potential but isn't so bent on winning that he forgets we're human."

There is no joy in losing.

cheapbooks/Shutterstock.com

97 Smile (a lot!)

It's simple: Athletes are more likely to be coachable and motivated when they see you smile, when you know all their names, and when you encourage them. Smiling means you are in a good mood, that you are content, that you are pleased with where you are and what you are doing. If kids can see that, it's easier to prompt them to want to be around you and participate in your sport. Smiling every day, in fact, should be a top priority for successful coaching. Through every season, you may come to depend more on a friendly, outward demeanor than any other skill or talent you have as a coach.

Because an intrinsic motivation for most young athletes is to gain approval from their peers and their coaches, they will constantly study your facial expressions and body language to determine how you are evaluating their progress. Your challenge, therefore, is to create the conditions in the practice room that capitalize on that intrinsic motivation by smiling and being friendly towards players.

You may have to work from dawn to dusk planning practices, repairing equipment, meeting with administrators, reviewing videos, instructing athletes and conducting drills, scouting opponents, and dialoging with parents. Such tasks can easily overwhelm even the most energetic person. But don't forget to smile!

And evaluate yourself at the end by totaling your number of successful relationships, not wins and losses. Creating these kinds of relationships depends first on knowing the interests and backgrounds of your athletes. To really motivate athletes, discover each one's background and show approval and acceptance for who they are and why they joined the team.

And don't forget to smile when they look at you.

Sasin Paraksa/Shutterstock.com

When their teenagers take the plunge into competitive sports, parents often expect the coach to be a special surrogate parent figure who can motivate like Vince Lombardi, teach like Socrates, and win like John Wooden. Such high expectations can make even the most confident person uncertain about becoming a coach.

Do you see yourself as a Tara Vanderveer or a Nick Saban? Should you use gimmicks and theatrics to motivate your athletes? Should today's coach act more like a cheerleader? Consider these questions when deciding how you want to motivate your players. Whatever strategies you eventually employ, be sure to maintain your own identity and style working with them. Second, gimmicks can be effective. if not overdone, and finally, you need, of course, to be supportive and involved as a coach but never lose your focus during a practice or game.

A school has its mission statement. A corporation has its company policy. A coach needs a personal philosophy. You can call it your personal beliefs or professional standards or private credo, it doesn't matter as long as you have one. That becomes your focus and your identity.

Just like parents who raise their children often in the same manner that they were raised, coaches often adopt the coaching style of the coach who coached them. This could be a mistake if that coach's personality or style does not match your own. Whatever strategies you eventually employ to achieve positive results with your athletes, be sure to maintain your own identity and style. Greg Shelley of the Janssen Sports Leadership Center is very direct about this issue: "Set a motivational 'standard' by what you do, say, and expect. Say it, expect it, but also make sure you do it!"

Whatever strategies you eventually employ to achieve positive results with your athletes, be sure to maintain your own identity and style.

Your coaching style is the summary of your personality when you enter the practice room or competition. It has little to do with what you wear and a lot to do with how you act and what you say. It is how your athletes know you and how they act when they're around you.

Your personality can have a major influence on the team's success and temperament. The *dictator's* philosophy is straightforward: "It's my way or the highway." In this instance, the head coach makes all the decisions and takes total control of the practice room environment. The athletes' duty is to follow through immediately to the head coach's demands. There are some serious faults to this approach. Dominique Stasulli in her article "How Coaches Contribute to Athletes' Motivation" cites important research on the *dictator's* influence on an athlete's motivation: "Controlling environments provide just the opposite: intimidation, reward manipulation, and negative regard for emotional influence on [the athlete's] performance."

The athlete may perform only for the praise of the coach or to avoid their anger. Although this is a very low-level way to motivate athletes, many coaches feel more comfortable with this role because they like being in control. Shelley has a warning: "First, instilling *fear* in others is simple (and it can quickly motivate some people), but over time, fear can easily breed resentment and disloyalty. The athlete who is motivated by fear is likely not so much trying to achieve something as they are trying to avoid something (e.g., losing a position or making a mistake). This athlete generally becomes focused on what not to do, rather than what to do. In time, this can become stressful and lead to a strong sense of resentment and/or disloyalty toward the one instilling the fear."

The *diplomat* coach, however, consults the athletes about rules and penalties. In this instance, the team establishes the conditions and consequences for group and individual behavior. You won't lose control or credibility by seeking their input. In fact, your athletes will be more motivated to follow you when you work *with* them in the formation of the rules that govern the team.

Diplomatic coaches involve the athletes at the first team meeting or at the first practice in arranging the rules the team needs to follow in order to achieve the goals they establish. The *diplomat* coach sees themselves as a partner with the athletes and as their teacher. Dr. Patricia Lucas, former principal of Manatee High School in Bradenton, Florida states, "I always hire a teacher who can coach rather than a coach who may or may not be a good teacher. The classroom performance must be credible first. Usually, an excellent teacher will be an excellent coach. Coaches occupy a unique position with students, often spending more time with them than their parents do. This opportunity to make a positive contribution to a young person's life is a serious responsibility."

Whether you choose to be a *dictator* or a *diplomat*, you need to remain consistent and fair with the athletes. Above all, you need to be yourself.

Be Creative 99

Coaches must create motivation much like an author composes an award-winning book or an artist paints on a canvas. The coach's best skills, insights, and efforts are required if effective motivation is the goal. Coaches need to give both creative and practical reflection on how they want to motivate their athletes in order to bring forth something within them that they didn't know they had. This requires careful planning and creative strategies.

"Always strive to be original and innovative in the application of motivational techniques," advises sports researcher Andrew Hamilton. "Each and every one of us has an untapped energy source that can be drawn upon to bring about superior results."

Coaches across the country continually try to gain an edge on the competition by building better facilities, purchasing state of the art equipment, and adding more personnel to their coaching staffs. All this can certainly make most teams more competitive, but coaches should consider more novel ways to motivate as much as they do the purchase of a blocking sled or a new wrestling mat.

Some coaches get creative with their schedule and travel across the country to compete and socialize with other schools in distant states. Other coaches try new ways to train or purchase new videos to show their teams. Some use the off-season for attending team-building camps or special events. You may choose to get creative with practice, with team introductions, or with p.a. announcements. Brainstorm the possibilities with your entire coaching staff and surprise your athletes.

Coaches must create motivation much like an author composes an award-winning book or an artist paints on a canvas.

The head coach, in short, leads by example. Your commitment, creativity, motivation, and effort establish the model that assistant coaches and athletes should follow. This is an awesome task.

5

The Post-Season

Brian A Jackson/Shutterstock.com

Host an Awards Program

100

Another major requirement for most coaches and a season-ending way to motivate players is an end-of-year awards program or banquet. At the beginning of the season, consult with the athletic director about your specific responsibilities in this regard. Early on, decide the type of awards you want to give out to your top athletes and the criteria that accompanies each award (see Figure 100-1 as an example).

Regarding awards, don't be afraid to share the wealth. In other words, use this event to honor and motivate as many different athletes as possible. It is also wise to allow the athletes to select (by private vote) the winner of at least one award. Typical awards could be the Most Improved Award (either from previous season to current season or from the beginning of the current season to its end), The Coach's Award (given to the hardest working and most coachable athlete), The Scholar-Athlete Award (for the most accomplished student, either by GPA or academic honors, on the team), and the Most Outstanding Athlete. Print this information and distribute it the parents and athletes at the beginning of the season, possibly at the "Meet the Team" program. Use this to motivate them from the git-go.

At this awards program, you might also choose to distribute T-shirts that declare any championships won by the team or trophies for athletes who were tops in certain statistical categories (for example, most tackles, most points, most individual victories, etc.). Also, acknowledge and thank all assistant coaches (including junior high or middle school coaches), the principal, assistant principal, athletic director, and trainers. Express gratitude to the school's booster club and other support groups (mention mothers and fathers by name), your statisticians, and any other personnel. Announce any tournament winners and all-conference, all-district, or all-state selections; reward the varsity letter winners; and finally hand out your major awards.

Since parents are in attendance, use the time again to explain your expectations of the athletes in the off-season. You may want them to attend a summer camp, participate in off-season conditioning sessions, compete in other school sports, or simply return some equipment or uniforms. Speak about their academics and their goals, the progress the team accomplished and the improvements that still need to come, the satisfaction you've had coaching, and the concerns you have for the upcoming season. Possibly, play a promotional video or hand out pictures taken of the athletes during the season by a school photographer. As in your first team meeting with the athletes, end on a positive note.

If organized effectively this awards program can be a very motivational event for your athletes and their parents and a positive way to end the season. Dr. Alan Goldberg affirms this notion when he says, "Recognition is one of the most powerful motivators there is."

EARNING A VARSITY LETTER

- For any player to earn a varsity letter they must compete in over one half of varsity games. Tournaments will count as two games. They must also compete in the sectional tournament.
- A player could receive a varsity letter, if the coaching staff feels this individual was an integral part of the team and did their best. They could, considering their level of ability and year of graduation.
- All players will be awarded junior varsity awards if they do not earn a varsity award.

AWARDS

The following trophies will be awarded:

Most Outstanding Player
- Given to the varsity player who advances farthest in the state tournament; who has the best won/loss record; who has the most tournament titles; and who has demonstrated a high level of technical superiority through the season.
- Determined by the vote of the coaching staff or at the coaches' discretion in case of injury at post-season tournaments.

Most Improved Player
- Given to the varsity player who shows the most development from the beginning to the end of the season; who increases their won/loss record to the positive side; who earns titles or awards during the latter part of the season after failing to do so early in the season; and whose skill level makes the most improvement.
- Determined by the vote of the coaching staff.

Most Outstanding Junior Varsity Player
- Given to the junior varsity player who has the best JV won/loss record; who earns the most tournament titles or place finishes; and who possibly competed successfully in some varsity competitions but did not earn a varsity letter.
- Determined by the vote of the coaching staff.

Coaches' Award
- Given to the senior player who displays the most service to the sport; who maintains daily a positive attitude; who demonstrates leadership; who has high attendance; and who dedicates themselves to improving their athletic skills.
- Determined by the vote of the coaching staff.

Hustle Award
- Given to the player either varsity or junior varsity who displays the most intensity and commitment throughout the season; who has the most enthusiasm and spirit; and who shows the most determination to excel, although their level of physical ability might be relatively limited.
- Determined by vote of the entire team.
- Note: this individual cannot also be a winner of any of the other major awards.

Figure 100-1. An example of post-season awards

Arrange a Beneficial Schedule

101

When scheduling, the coach should arrange competitions, especially tournaments, where players can compete at their level and abilities. That said, when scheduling competitions for the junior high and high school programs, be sure to compete against at least two schools outside your conference schedule whose players' skill level are comparable to your own team and at least two teams where you feel confident about success. This enables most athletes to be successful and to maintain their confidence (and motivation). Then, schedule two superior teams in order to expose the players to the characteristics of winning programs: their aggressive style of play, their conditioning, their fan support. To be sure, do not include more than two teams like this for either the junior high or high school schedule, since you don't want to damage the confidence (and motivation) of your athletes too easily.

You can also arrange, after receiving permission from your administration, a competition that requires your team to travel a significant distance and stay overnight. Athletes enjoy the special status and experience of traveling to a distant school and staying in hotel rooms or with host families for a game or tournament. This could certainly be a highlight for their season and add to their motivation.

Another key element to proper scheduling is to avoid any conflicts with your school's other programs. Set the starting times to promote large attendance by parents and students. Be sure that your junior high athletes can attend your high school competitions for free and have your high school athletes attend, as a group, at least one junior high competition.

When scheduling, the coach should arrange competitions, especially tournaments, where players can compete at their level and abilities.

iQoncept/Shutterstock.com

About the Author

Keith Manos is a former wrestling coach who, in 2009, was inducted into the Ohio Wrestling Coaches Hall of Fame, after a successful coaching tenure that includes being named Ohio Wrestling Coach of the Year in 1988, head coach of the USA All Star Wrestling Team in 1989, and head coach of the Ohio All-Star Wrestling Team in 1991. The Greater Cleveland Wrestling Coaches and Officials Association awarded Keith their Coach of the Year award in 1989 and their Award of Merit in 2002. In addition, the Ohio High School Athletic Association honored Keith with their State Award in 2013. In 2000, Keith was designated as Ohio's High School English Teacher of the Year by the Ohio Council of Teachers of English and Language Arts, was named Who's Who of American High School Teachers in 2005, and was inducted into the National Honor Roll of Outstanding American Teachers in 2006.

Keith has written several other books, including *Wrestling Coaches Survival Guide* (1995) and *Writing Smarter* (1998), both of which were published by Prentice Hall. Coaches Choice subsequently published five more of his books, most recently *The Elite Wrestler* (2021). In addition, Keith has authored numerous articles and stories for coaches which have appeared in national publications like *Scholastic Coach*, *Wesleyan Advocate*, *School Library Journal*, *Teacher Magazine*, *Athletic Management*, and *Wrestling USA*, among others.